THE AUSTRALIAN
FINANCIAL REVIEW

DICTIONARY
OF INVESTMENT TERMS

from COUNTY NATWEST

THE AUSTRALIAN

FINANCIAL REVIEW

DICTIONARY

OF INVESTMENT TERMS

from COUNTY NATWEST

FOURTH EDITION

THE AUSTRALIAN
FINANCIAL REVIEW

A publication of AFR Books
a publishing division of John Fairfax Publications Pty Ltd ACN 003 357 720

AFR Books is a member of Publish Australia

Managing editor: Sarah Hodgkinson
Publishing consultant: Ann Atkinson

First three editions published by County NatWest 1989–1994
as the *County NatWest Dictionary of Investment Terms*
This fourth edition published 1996, reprinted 1996

Printed in Australia by McPhersons Printing Group, Victoria
Typeset by DOCUPRO, Sydney
Cover Design: Jackie Francis and Jennifer Barrett

National Library of Australia Cataloguing-in-Publication data

The Australian Financial Review dictionary of investment terms from
County NatWest

4th ed.
ISBN 1 86290 108 2.

1. Finance—Dictionaries. 2. Investments—Dictionaries. I. Australian Financial
Review. II. County NatWest Australia Investment Management Ltd. III. Title: Dictionary
of investment terms from County NatWest. IV. Title: Dictionary of investment terms.

332.603

COUNTY NATWEST

Investment Management

County NatWest is delighted to publish this fourth edition of its *Dictionary of Investment Terms* in conjunction with *The Australian Financial Review*.

First published in 1989, the Dictionary commenced its life as a reference source for County NatWest's clients, but has since evolved into a benchmark publication for the broader financial community in Australia. Our motivation in making the Dictionary more widely available, in partnership with Australia's premier financial newspaper, reflects the increasing demand we have experienced for its practical and relevant explanation of commonly used expressions, terms, abbreviations and acronyms used in the investment industry.

Since the first edition, the number of definitions included in the Dictionary has quadrupled, testimony to the increasing complexity and breadth of the investment business. That complexity is intrinsically unhealthy, for If the people who engage or study the behaviour of investment managers cannot understand the language used by those professionals, the managers themselves cannot expect to clearly communicate their strategies. And in business, nothing is more dangerous than misunderstood communication.

The Dictionary does not purport to be a textbook on economics or portfolio theory. Rather we have sought to prepare a layperson's definition of the terms which are regularly used within the industry as an aid to wider understanding. For this fourth edition we have added a number of new terms which reflect the continued pace of regulatory change, new product development and refinements to management practices in our industry. It also reflects our commitment to keeping the Dictionary as up to date and relevant a reference source for all readers as we can.

The contributions to the Dictionary, while all written in-house, are the result of decades of thinking and argument about investment markets and asset management by professionals and academics around the world. Inevitably, there will be disagreements with some definitions and some others we have omitted to include. We would welcome your comments, criticisms and suggestions for future editions. We hope you find the Dictionary useful.

Nick Birrell
Chief Executive Officer

May 1996

AARF Abbreviation for *Australian Accounting Research Foundation.*

AAS Abbreviation for *Australian Accounting Standards.* See *Accounting Standards.*

AAS25 Abbreviation for **Australian Accounting Standard No. 25** entitled Financial Reporting by Superannuation Plans. Under this standard, accounts for certain superannuation funds are required to include valuations of assets at net market value rather than cost.

AASB Abbreviation for *Australian Accounting Standards Board.*

ABS Abbreviation for *Australian Bureau of Statistics.*

ACCC Abbreviation for *Australian Competition and Consumer Commission.*

Acceptor The party to whom a *Bill of Exchange* is addressed, and who accepts primary liability to pay on maturity the face value of the bill to its holder. See also *Bank Bill.*

Accord Commonly-used shorthand for the **Prices and Incomes Accord,** a series of agreements between the Australian Government and the trade union movement since the early 1980s concerning salaries and benefits (including superannuation) to be provided to Australian workers under industrial awards.

Accounting Standards

Accounting Standards   Practice notes and policies issued by the *Australian Accounting Research Foundation* setting out acceptable practices and procedures for adoption by accountants and auditors. Australian Accounting Standards are usually abbreviated to AAS and numbered (eg. *AAS25*), and are adhered to by the professional accounting associations (ie. *Australian Society of Certified Practising Accountants* and *Institute of Chartered Accountants in Australia*).

Accrual Accounting   An accounting methodology which takes account of accrued as well as actual expenses and revenue during the relevant accounting period. For example, if interest payments on a bond owned by an investor are building up but have not yet been paid, the amount notionally built up at the time of accounting is included in accruals, even though it has not actually been received. (See also *Cash Accounting*).

Accrued Benefits   In relation to superannuation, the benefits which have already accumulated at a given point in time, as distinct from those which may or will build up in the future.

Accrued Interest   Interest earned on a security or bank deposit but not yet paid.

Accumulated Interest   Periodic interest payments which are past due and unpaid.

Accumulation Fund   Another term for *Defined Contribution Fund*.

Accumulation Index   A numerical index of movement in a financial market, which takes account of both price movement *(capital)* and income *(dividends)*. Investment performance should generally be measured against an accumulation index rather than a price index, which measures movements in price only (not income). (See also *All Ordinaries Accumulation Index*).

Active Management   A style of investment management which seeks to attain returns above a set benchmark by *asset allocation* and *stock selection*. (Opposite of *Passive Management*).

Active Market   A market in which the volume of securities traded is heavy or above normal.

Active Position   The difference between the actual level of investment made in a particular asset class and the *benchmark* level of investment in that asset class.

ACTU   Abbreviation for *Australian Council of Trade Unions.*

Actual Price   The price at which a deal for the transfer of ownership of an asset is formally completed, eg. in a share transaction. (Not to be confused with *Closing Price*).

Actuarial Value   The present value of a *defined benefit* superannuation fund as determined by an actuary, taking account of current assets and expected future contributions, together with expected future benefits payments, discounted by appropriate interest factors.

Actuary A professional person qualified to make calculations and valuations in respect of superannuation funds, insurance funds or other forms of investment. Actuaries apply mathematical, statistical, economic and financial analysis to a wide range of practical business problems, with particular emphasis on longer term financial contracts involving the need to incorporate assessment of risk or uncertain financial outcomes. Actuaries operating in Australia are normally qualified as Fellows of the *Institute of Actuaries of Australia.*

ADCAL Abbreviation for *Australian Development Capital Association Limited.*

ADF Abbreviation for Approved Deposit Fund.

Administrator a) A person appointed by a court to administer the estate of a person who has died without leaving a will, or where the appointed executor is unable or unwilling to perform the task; b) a person appointed by a regulatory authority in certain circumstances to take charge of the affairs of a company or financial institution in place of the Board of Directors. (See also Liquidator, Receiver); or c) in relation to superannuation funds, the individual or company responsible for the day to day operation of the fund.

AFIC Abbreviation for *Australian Financial Institutions Commission.*

AFMA Abbreviation for *Australian Financial Markets Association.*

Age Dependency Ratio A statistical measure of the ratio of persons above retirement age to those below retirement age. The ratio is commonly used as a leading indicator of the projected ageing rate of the general population.

Agent A person employed to act on behalf of another (a principal).

Aggressive Portfolio A portfolio which is significantly different from the index (or its benchmark) and which is designed to provide above-average returns by taking above-average risk. Typically, such portfolios have a relatively high exposure to *equity* investments.

AGM Abbreviation for *Annual General Meeting*.

AIMA Abbreviation for *Australian Investment Managers' Association*.

AIST Abbreviation for *Australian Institute of Superannuation Trustees*.

All Industrials Index See *All Ordinaries Index*.

Allocated Pension A type of retirement income arrangement under which an individual invests a lump sum and then draws down an annual pension to a value he/she sees fit, taking account of his/her own expected cash flow needs and life expectancy. If the drawdown is greater than investment earnings, then part of the initial capital sum is used to make up the difference. Unlike a traditional pension or annuity, an allocated pension can therefore provide the retiree with continual access to the capital sum invested, and allows any balance to be passed on to beneficiaries upon the death of the individual concerned. Also called **Cash Back Pension**.

Allocation Price The price at which a unit in a *unit trust* is issued. Also known as **Purchase Price**. (Opposite of *Redemption Price*).

All Ordinaries Accumulation Index An *accumulation index* measuring movements in both the price (capital) and dividends (income) of the major shares listed on the *Australian Stock Exchange*. (See also *All Ordinaries Index*).

All Ordinaries Accumulation Index 1980-1995

All Ordinaries Index   A share price index measuring the market prices of the major stocks listed on the *Australian Stock Exchange*. The index is calculated continuously, and expressed as a number which allows overall market fluctuations to be quickly gauged (eg. if the index was at 2000 at a given point in time and the overall value of the shares concerned rose by 10%, then the index would rise to 2200). Note that not all of the companies listed on the Australian Stock Exchange make up the All Ordinaries Index. Note also that the Index is broken into a series of sub-indices including the **All Resources, All Industrials,** the **50 Leaders** and a series of sector indices such as mining, media, transport, etc.

All Resources Index   See *All Ordinaries Index*.

Alpha   The return a security or a portfolio would be expected to earn if the market rate of return were zero. A positive alpha indicates that an investment has earned on average a premium above that expected for the level of market variability. A negative alpha would indicate that the investment received on average a premium lower than that expected for the level of market variability. Sometimes alpha is used as a performance indicator. (See also *Beta, Delta*).

ALRC   Abbreviation for *Australian Law Reform Commission.*

AMBA   Abbreviation for *Australian Merchant Bankers' Association.*

American Option   An option which may be exercised any time between its initiation and expiration dates (inclusive). American options are among those traded on the floor of the *Sydney Futures Exchange*. (See also *European Option*).

Amortisation Paying off an interest bearing liability by gradual reduction through a series of installments comprising both principal and interest components, as opposed to paying it off by a single lump-sum payment. A technique for gradually extinguishing a liability or capital expenditure over a period of time (eg. as in a typical home mortgage). (See also *Credit Foncier Loan*).

Amortised Yield See *Yield*.

Analyst A trained person who investigates all the facts concerning a security or industry under study and reaches a dependable conclusion about its merits that may help an investor to decide what action he or she should take.

Annual Accounts A yearly summary of the financial position of a company or superannuation fund. Typically includes a *balance sheet* and *profit and loss account*.

Annual Benefit Statement A report from the manager or trustees of a superannuation fund, advising members of details of their accrued and future benefits in a fund.

Annual General Meeting (AGM) The yearly meeting between the directors and shareholders of a company, at which shareholders are asked to elect the directors, discuss any shareholder resolutions and approve the operating and financial results of the past year.

Annualising The expression of a rate of return over periods other than a year converted to annual terms. For example, a compound return of 21% over two years would convert into an annualised return of 10% per annum, even though each annual return looked nothing like 10%. For example, if an investment earned minus 2% in year one and 23.5% in year two, the compound annual return would be 10%. (See also *Compounding*).

Annuity An arrangement under which periodic payments are made to a person in return for the investment of a lump sum, usually for the purpose of providing retirement income. (See also *Allocated Pension, Deferred Annuity*).

Anticipatory Hedging The taking of a *futures* position to hedge an anticipated position in the market for the underlying physical security.

APEC Abbreviation for *Asia-Pacific Economic Co-operation Group*.

Appreciation a) Generally, an increase in the value of an asset; b) In relation to foreign exchange transactions, the rise in the value of a currency in terms of another currency or currencies.

Approved Deposit Fund (ADF) A type of fund into which *Eligible Termination Payments* can be 'rolled over' upon a person's retirement, resignation or retrenchment. ADFs were introduced in 1984 following changes to the tax laws affecting lump-sum superannuation payouts, as a means of ensuring that payments intended for retirement purposes continue to attract favourable taxation treatment. (See also *Annuity*).

Approved Trustee   An organisation eligible to be the trustee of a *Public Offer Fund* under the SIS Legislation. An Approved Trustee must be a corporation, fulfil certain capital/net asset or custodial requirements, and have been approved by the *Insurance and Superannuation Commission* as being capable of properly performing the trustee's duties. Approved Trustee status only applies to trusteeships of Public Offer Funds; it should be distinguished from the requirements of a *corporate trustee* for a regular employer sponsored superannuation fund.

Arbitrage   Taking advantage of countervailing prices in different markets – eg. the purchase of an asset for a low price in one market and its sale for a higher price in another.

Arbitrageur   A person who engages in *arbitrage*.

Arithmetic Average   In the context of investment performance surveys, a "simple" average of the sum of all values measured, divided by the number of those values. As opposed to the *asset-weighted average*.

Arm's Length   A description of a transaction conducted on a strictly commercial basis. The term is used particularly in cases where the parties to the transaction are associated with each other (ie. to ensure that the transaction proceeds as if the parties were completely independent of each other).

Arrears   a) In the case of superannuation, contributions which are overdue; b) More generally, the term refers to money which is now due, but has not yet been paid.

Articles of Association   A document which spells out the internal rules of operation of a company. (See also *Memorandum of Association*).

ASA   Abbreviation for *Australian Shareholders' Association*.

ASAC Abbreviation for **Asian Securities Analysts Council.**

ASC Abbreviation for *Australian Securities Commission.*

ASCT Abbreviation for *Australian Society of Corporate Treasurers.*

ASFA Abbreviation for **Association of Superannuation Funds of Australia.** A national industry association established in 1961 to promote the interests of superannuation funds and their trustees and members.

Asian Securities Analysts Council (ASAC) An international co-operative organisation for securities analysts in the Asian and Oceania regions. The purpose of ASAC is to promote the interchange of securities analysis and fund management expertise on matters of common interest to member associations (including the *Securities Institute of Australia*).

Asia-Pacific Economic Co-Operation Group (APEC) An international grouping of nations in the Pacific, East Asia and North America established to advance regional interests and promote free trade policies around the world. APEC commenced as the Asia Pacific Economic Forum in 1989, but rose to greater prominence in November 1993 when leaders of most member nations met in Seattle, United States to formalise their combined regional policies and trade principles. The founding membership of APEC comprises Australia, Brunei, Canada, China, Hong Kong, Indonesia, Japan, Malaysia, New Zealand, the Philippines, Singapore, South Korea, Taiwan, Thailand and the United States – a grouping of nations representing approximately 40% of the world's population, 40% of the world's trade, and 50% of global *gross domestic product.*

Ask Price   The price at which the holder of a security is prepared to sell that security. (See also *Offer*).

Asset Allocation   The apportionment of an investment portfolio among different asset classes *(shares, bonds, property, cash* and overseas investments) from time to time in accordance with the investment outlook of the investor or investment manager. Also known as **Investment Mix**. (See also *Strategic Asset Allocation* and *Tactical Asset Allocation*).

Asset Allocation Model   A computer model which, given information and forecasts for the various asset classes *(return, risk, covariances)*, will give asset allocations which will be most efficient in terms of the trade-off between risk and return. (See also *Optimisation*).

Asset Backing   The value of a company's assets standing behind its issued shares. Some companies may have a strong asset backing even if the dividends they pay on shares are relatively low. (See also *Net Asset Backing*).

Asset Class   A broadly defined category of financial assets (eg. domestic shares, overseas bonds, cash, etc).

Asset Consultant   A professional person engaged by investors such as superannuation fund trustees to advise on appropriate investment strategies, asset allocation and selection of investment managers.

Assets   The resources owned by a company, fund or individual. Cash, investments, money due, materials and inventories are called *current assets;* buildings and machinery are known as *fixed assets;* and patents and goodwill are known *as intangible assets.* Opposite of *liabilities.*

Asset Value   The value of the assets underpinning a security. These may not be fully reflected in the price of a security. (See also *Net Asset Value*).

Asset-Weighted Average   In the context of investment performance surveys, an average derived by comparing returns earned by fund managers where those returns are weighted according to the managers' respective size of assets under management. An alternative to the use of *arithmetic averages.*

Assignment   The transfer of property (eg. an assignment of interest under a will, an assignment of rights in a patent or an assignment of a lease or mortgage). An assignment of contract is an act by which one person substitutes another as a party to a contract, either for some or all of the purposes of the contract. The assignment of rights and liabilities under contracts is limited by law.

Assurance   Traditionally used to describe insurance based on human life (hence 'life assurance').

ASX   Abbreviation for *Australian Stock Exchange.*

Asymmetric Hedge   An option-based *hedge.* 'Asymmetric' refers to the fact that the protection afforded by an option-based hedge will not be symmetrical, because the return from a call option is not as great as the return would have been from investing in the *underlying security* directly.

At a Discount   Below par value. A security is said to be selling at a discount when the market value is below the par value of the security. Shares can also be said to be trading at a discount (or premium) to *net tangible assets.*

At a Premium   Above *par Value*. A security is said to be selling at a premium when its market price is above its par value.

ATO   Abbreviation for *Australian Taxation Office*.

At Par   The price which equals the face value (*par value*) of a security.

At the Close   Describing an order calling for execution of an order at the price obtainable 'at the close' of the market on the day it is entered.

At the Market   Describing an order which the broker will execute at the best price obtainable at the moment he or she receives it on the trading floor. Synonymous with *market order*. (See also *Limit Order*).

At the Money   Referring to a *call option* or a *put option* whose *exercise price* is equal (or virtually equal) to the current price of the commodity or asset on which the option is written.

At the Opening   Describing an order to be executed at the best price obtainable as soon as the market opens: no actual price limit is set.

Attribution Analysis   The process by which the return on an investment portfolio is attributed to its manager's investment decisions. Typically the decisions in respect of which performance is attributed are *stock selection*, *asset allocation* and *market timing*.

Audit An independent examination of the records and operations of a company, superannuation fund or other legal entity to check on compliance with accounting requirements and/or regulatory standards. A conventional financial audit is conducted to scrutinise the annual accounts of an organisation to ascertain whether (in the opinion of the auditor) they represent a true and fair view of the organisation's financial status. Other types of audits might be conducted at the initiation of management or regulatory authorities; for example, audits of an organisation's information technology systems. Under the *SIS Legislation,* audit requirements include examination of a fund's compliance with prescribed operating standards, such as the requirement that funds do not lend money to their members. (See also *External Audit* and *Internal Audit).*

Ausmaq Derived from **Australian Market Automated Quotation System,** Ausmaq is an on-line transaction network designed primarily for financial advisers but also investors and fund managers. It facilitates automated transaction processes for the issue and redemption of units in public *unit trusts.*

AUSSIE MAC A mortgage-backed certificate issued by the *National Mortgage Market Corporation,* first issued in 1985. (See also *Securitisation).*

Austraclear A computerised settlement and safe custody system for *bills of exchange* and, more recently, cash transactions. Austraclear records trades and changes of ownership and removes the need for bills of exchange or cash to physically change hands.

Australian Accounting Research Foundation (AARF) The organisation which researches and issues *accounting standards* for Australian practitioners. Founded in 1966, the AARF is jointly sponsored by the *Australian Society of Certified Practising Accountants* and the *Institute of Chartered Accountants in Australia*.

Australian Accounting Standard No. 25 See *AAS25*.

Australian Accounting Standards Board (AASB) A Board established under the *Corporations Law* to develop a conceptual framework for evaluating proposed accounting standards, and to review, sponsor, consult upon or change proposed standards.

Australian Bureau of Statistics (ABS) The Commonwealth Government body responsible for the collection and publication of statistical data on a wide range of matters, including economics, demographic trends and census figures.

Australian Competition and Consumer Commission (ACCC) The Commonwealth Government agency responsible for administering legislation concerning fair trade practices, prices surveillance, competition and consumer protection. It was formed in 1995 by merging of the former *Trade Practices Commission* and *Prices Surveillance Authority*.

Australian Council of Trade Unions (ACTU) The national organisation for Australia's trade union movement. The ACTU was established in 1927 and has its headquarters in Melbourne.

Australian Development Capital Association Limited (ADCAL) An industry association formed in April 1992 for specialist managers, investors and other participants in Australia's *development capital* industry.

Australian Financial Institutions Commission (AFIC) The body established by uniform legislation among the states and territories to regulate the affairs of Australia's *non-bank financial institutions*. AFIC commenced its operations on 1 July 1992.

Australian Financial Markets Association (AFMA) A national industry body for organisations in over-the-counter (OTC) financial markets. As an industry association, AFMA membership represents almost 200 organisations, large and small, comprising the full range of participants in wholesale financial markets. The AFMA mandate includes facilitation, consultation and dissemination on issues including benchmarking, self-regulation, market risk, dispute resolution, market conventions, codes of conduct, education, documentation and access to better quality information through AFMA*data*.

AFMA

Australian Institute of Superannuation Trustees (AIST)
An institute founded in June 1992 by the
Conference of Major Superannuation Funds to
represent the interests of superannuation fund
trustees. The AIST is an independent, non-profit
incorporated association, whose objectives include
the promotion of ethical and effective performance
standards by trustees, improvement of the
knowledge and skills of trustees, representations to
government and relevant authorities on matters of
concern to trustees, and enhancement of sound
management and security of superannuation funds
by trustees on behalf of their members. The
Institute's information and educational activities
include provision of a reference manual to
members as well as access to an ongoing seminar
series.

Australian Investment Managers' Association (AIMA)   An industry association formed in December 1990 to promote the interests of institutional fund managers and to propose measures to improve the efficiency and integrity of Australian capital markets. Among the activities of the AIMA are the issue of practice notes recommending appropriate actions for institutional investors on corporate governance issues, the preparation of submissions to government on fund management regulatory issues, liaison with overseas institutional shareholder and funds management associations, and advice to companies in understanding the requirements of institutional investors. As at December 1995 the AIMA had 62 members, representing combined funds under management of approximately $320 billion.

AIMA

Australian Investment Managers' Association

Australian Law Reform Commission (ALRC)   A Commonwealth Government body responsible for reforms on legal issues referred to it by the Attorney-General. Together with the *Companies and Securities Advisory Committee,* the ALRC was responsible for a major review of Australia's collective investments industry in 1992–94, leading to a number of expected legislative changes during 1996.

Australian Market Automated Quotation System   See *Ausmaq.*

Australian Merchant Bankers' Association (AMBA) An industry association representing participants in Australia's wholesale banking, securities and financial markets. AMBA's membership comprises both Australian and foreign-owned institutions including the operations of major international and investment banks which operate in Australia.

Australian Ratings Australia's only home-grown credit rating agency, based in Melbourne. Now owned by Standard & Poors. (See also *Moody's, Standard & Poors*).

Australian Securities Commission (ASC) The Commonwealth Government body responsible for regulation of companies and the securities and futures industries under the *Corporations Law*. The ASC commenced its operations on 1 January 1991, replacing the *National Companies and Securities Commission* and State Corporate Affairs Commissions which existed under the previous co-operative scheme of companies and securities regulation. (See also *Australian Accounting Standards Board, Companies Auditors and Liquidation Disciplinary Board*).

AUSTRALIAN
SECURITIES
COMMISSION

Australian Society of Certified Practising Accountants (ASCPA) Formerly known as the Australian Society of Accountants. One of the two main professional associations for the accounting profession in Australia. (See also *Institute of Chartered Accountants in Australia*).

Australian Society of Corporate Treasurers (ASCT) A national professional organisation established in 1986, representing 1130 corporate and public sector treasury professionals. The ASCT aims to provide forums for the discussion of treasury issues, provide education to members and keep members involved and informed on submissions to Government. The head office is in Melbourne.

Australian Stock Exchange (ASX) The national organisation for dealing in shares, bonds and certain other securities. The Australian Stock Exchange Limited commenced operations in 1987, replacing the previous State-based exchanges.

AUSTRALIAN STOCK EXCHANGE
LIMITED

Authorised Capital The maximum number of shares, valued at their par value, which a company is permitted to issue under its rules. (See also *Issued Capital*).

Authorised Dealers A select group of companies which make up the 'official' short term *money market* in Australia. Authorised dealers are utilised by the *Reserve Bank of Australia* for investment of short term cash surpluses and to stimulate trade in government securities.

Authorised Foreign Exchange Dealers   Organisations granted a general authority by the Government to buy and sell foreign currency in Australia under the Banking (Foreign Exchange) Regulations.

Authorised Investments   The investments which a *pooled investment* fund is permitted to make, eg. under the fund's *Trust Deed*.

Automatic Exercise   The exercise by the clearing house of an *in-the-money option* at expiration, unless the holder of the option has submitted specific instructions to the contrary.

Average Price   The mean, or average, price obtained in the purchase or sale of a block of securities.

Average Rate Option   An *option* structured in such a way as to allow traders to hedge their daily exposures using a single contract which covers the entire period of that exposure.

Average Weekly Earnings (AWE)   A measure of wage and salary levels of employees in Australia, published monthly by the *Australian Bureau of Statistics*. AWE is one of the key measures used by economists to assess the state of the economy, particularly to gauge the overall level of activity and potential inflationary influences. (See also *Average Weekly Ordinary Time Earnings*).

Average Weekly Ordinary Time Earnings (AWOTE)
Similar to *Average Weekly Earnings* except that overtime earnings are excluded, making it a less volatile measure in the short term but a less accurate measure in the long term.

Averaging Up or Down   The practice of purchasing the same security at various price levels, thereby arriving at a higher or lower average cost.

Award An industrial agreement between employers and employees, ratified by a State or Commonwealth Industrial Tribunal, setting out salary levels and terms and conditions of employment.

Award Superannuation Superannuation entitlements which are paid to an employee pursuant to an industrial *award*. (See also *Industry Funds*).

AWE Abbreviation for *Average Weekly Earnings*.

AWOTE Abbreviation for *Average Weekly Ordinary Time Earnings*.

Back-End Load   See *Redemption Fee*.

Back Office   See *Front Office*.

Back Spread   In *options* trading, a position in which more options are purchased than sold, and where all options have the same underlying security and expire at the same time. Back spreads usually have a neutral *delta*.

Backwardation   A situation which occasionally occurs in *futures* or *options* markets, whereby current commodities or contracts with an earlier maturity date have a higher value than contracts with a later maturity date. (Opposite of *Contango*).

Badged Product   An investment product that is administered and/or managed by one organisation, but labelled with the name of another organisation which is typically responsible for distribution of the product.

BAD Tax   Aptly named abbreviation for **Bank Accounts Debit Tax**, a federal government tax on withdrawals from bank accounts by cheque.

Balance Date   The completion of an accounting period – typically 30 June for the majority of Australian companies and superannuation funds.

Balanced Fund   An investment portfolio which diversifies its holdings over a range of asset classes which typically include shares, fixed interest, property, overseas securities and cash.

Balanced Manager   An investment manager whose expertise includes *asset allocation* and the supervision of portfolios containing a variety of classes of investments (as distinct from expertise in managing a particular asset class such as shares). (See also *Specialist Manager*).

Balance of Payments   A record of a nation's position in relation to financial transactions with all other nations. Balance of Payments figures are made up of both *current account* items (eg. imports and exports) and *capital account* items (eg. borrowings and investments). In Australia, Balance of Payments figures are published monthly by the *Australian Bureau of Statistics*.

Balance Sheet   A key financial statement showing the nature and amount of a company's assets, liabilities and capital on a given date. In one column all the company's assets are listed with their values, and in the other all its liabilities and the equity of the shareholders. (See also *Profit and Loss Account*).

Balloon Payment   The final payment terminating a debt, in which the amount paid is substantially more than previous instalments.

Bank Bill   A *Bill of Exchange* of which the *acceptor* and/or *endorser* is a bank. If the bank is the acceptor, the bill is known as a **bank accepted bill**. If the bank is the endorser, the bill is known as a **bank endorsed bill**.

Banker's Acceptance   An American term for a *Bank Accepted Bill*. Used in domestic and/or international trade or commerce to finance the shipment and storage of goods or to facilitate currency exchange transactions with foreign banks. A popular money market investment.

Bankers' Blanket Bond Insurance   A form of insurance taken out by a fund manager against losses incurred from the negligence or fraudulent activity of an employee. Also called a **Blanket Fidelity Bond**.

Bank of England   The *central bank* of the United Kingdom. The bank was established privately in 1694 and was nationalised by the British Parliament in 1946.

Bankruptcy   A declaration by the Federal Court to place all of an individual's assets and liabilities with an official receiver to liquidate and distribute to creditors, according to prescribed legal guidelines. Bankruptcy can be declared if an individual's liabilities exceed his or her assets and/or accounts can not be paid. It should be noted that bankruptcy applies to an individual; the equivalent status for a corporation is *receivership* or *liquidation*.

BARRA   Software programs developed by the international investment consulting firm Barra International used to evaluate risk profiles, chiefly in equity investments.

Barrier Option   A conventional *option* which cannot be exercised above or below a specified price. If the price of the underlying security moved outside this specified price range during the life of the option, the option cannot be exercised.

Basis   The price difference between the actual or spot commodity and derivative market valuations. (See also *Basis Risk*).

Basis Point   A measurement of fluctuation of an investment, equal to 1/100 of one percent.

Basis Risk The extent to which valuations for *derivative* securities do not accurately reflect valuations for the underlying physical securities on which they are based. Basis risk is sometimes exploited by investors engaged in *index arbitrage*.

Basket Option An *option* constructed around a series (or "basket") of different commodities, securities or currencies. For example, a currency basket option gives its holder the right to buy (call) or sell (put) a specified basket of foreign currencies in exchange for a fixed price (denominated in the investor's native currency) at a specified future date. Currency basket options have become prominent in modern portfolio management practices, as they allow investors to hedge all or most of their foreign currencies simultaneously, often at lower cost than would be incurred for individual option contracts on each currency.

Bear Someone who believes the market will decline. (Opposite of *Bull*).

Bearer Bond A bond made payable to its holder (bearer).

Bear Market A market in which prices decline sharply against a background of widespread pessimism. The opposite of *Bull Market*. Bear markets are generally shorter in duration than bull markets.

Bear Spread In relation to *options* markets, any *spread* in which a decline in the price of the underlying asset will theoretically increase the value of the spread. (Opposite of *Bull Spread*).

Below Par A price below the face value *(par value)* of a security.

Benchmark An index or other market measurement which is used by a fund manager as a yardstick to assess the risk and performance of a portfolio. For example, the *All Ordinaries Accumulation Index* is a commonly used benchmark for Australian share portfolios.

Benchmark Portfolio A model portfolio which is developed to provide a standard for measuring the manager's risk/ return performance, and to reflect the investor's preferred level of risk over a complete market cycle. A benchmark portfolio will typically include individual sector indices as benchmarks for each asset class held within the portfolio.

Beneficial Interest The entitlement to receive benefits generated by assets held in another party's name, such as a *Trustee*. (See also *Beneficiary*).

Beneficiary The person or organisation which is entitled to receive the benefits generated by an asset, where the asset is legally registered in the name of another party, such as a *Trustee*.

Benefit In relation to superannuation, the entitlement (eg. *pension, lump sum, annuity*) received by the member after his or her employment has ceased.

Beta   A measure of market-sensitivity – ie. the extent to which a share or a portfolio fluctuates with the market. Beta is a statistical estimate, based on historical data, of the average percentage change in a fund's or a security's rate of return corresponding to a one percent change in the market. For example, a security (or portfolio) with a beta of 1.2 might be expected to perform some 20% better than the market when it rises, and 20% worse when it falls. Similarly, a beta of 0.5% implies a movement equal to only half the market's rise or fall. (See also *Alpha*).

Bid   The price offered for a commodity, currency or investment instrument which is desired to be purchased.

Bid-Asked   Often referred to as a **quotation** or **quote**. The *bid* is the highest price anyone has indicated that he or she will pay for a security at a given time, and the *asked* is the lowest price anyone will accept at the same time. Also known as **Bid-Offer**.

Bid Price   The highest quoted price that any prospective buyer will pay for a security at a particular point in time. The 'bid price' is the actual market price for a share, regardless of the price of the last sale.

Bid Rate   The exchange rate at which bank is willing to buy a currency in exchange for another.

Bill of Exchange   An unconditional order in writing requiring the party to whom it is addressed to pay a certain sum on a fixed date in the future. Bills of exchange are *negotiable instruments*, usually maturing within six months, and sold at a discount to face value. The party to whom the bill is addressed, and who accepts it, is known as the *acceptor* and assumes primary liability to pay on maturity the face value of the bill to its holder. The *drawer* who issues the bill is liable should the acceptor fail to pay. If the bill has been endorsed by a third party, such as a bank, the *endorser* is liable should both the acceptor and the drawer fail to pay. See also *Bank Bill*.

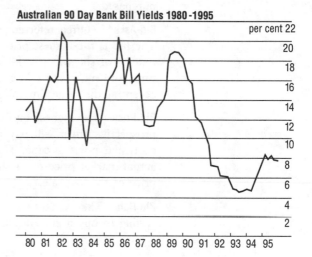

Australian 90 Day Bank Bill Yields 1980-1995

Black & Scholes Model   A mathematical model used for valuation of *options* to determine whether the current trading price is an accurate valuation of the option. The model was developed in the early 1980s by American mathematicians Fischer Black and Myron Scholes.

Block A large holding or transaction of shares. Also known as a **Block Trade.**

Blue Chip Referring to the shares of a leading company which is known for excellent management and a strong financial structure. The term has become a generic one for quality securities.

Bond A *debt security* issued by such entities as corporations, governments or their agencies (eg. *statutory authorities*). A bond holder is a creditor of the issuer and not a shareholder.

Bond Interest Coverage A measure of bond safety, calculated by dividing total income by the annual interest on bonds.

Bond Ratings A system for measuring the relative creditworthiness of bond issues using rating symbols, which range from the highest investment quality (least investment risk) to the lowest investment quality (greatest risk). (See also *Investment Grade Bonds*).

Bond Tender A procedure for selling bonds through the seeking of written bids from institutions. In Australia, sales of Commonwealth bonds have occurred through a periodic tender system since the early 1980s.

Bonus Shares Shares issued free by a corporation to its existing shareholders on a pro rata entitlement basis.

Books Closing Date The date a share registry is closed off after the declaration of a dividend, for the determining of the amount to be paid to each shareholder.

Book Value The net dollar value at which an asset or security is carried on a balance sheet. In portfolio accounting, book value generally refers to the price paid for the security, as opposed to its current worth or *market value*.

Bottom See *Trough*.

Bottom-up Analysis A form of *security analysis* which begins with forecasting returns for individual companies, then moves to industries and finally the economy as a whole. (Opposite of *Top-down Forecasting*).

Bourse A vernacular term for a stock exchange, derived from the French word meaning 'purse'.

Box A package of *options* comprising a long *call* and short *put* at one *exercise price*, and a short call and long put option at a different exercise price. All four options making up the 'box' have the same underlying asset and expire at the same time.

Bracket Creep The movement of peoples' wages into higher tax brackets as a result of wage increases.

Broad Money The widest of various measures used to gauge the growth of a nations' *money supply*. It includes all holdings of notes and coin by the public, as well as borrowings by *non-bank financial institutions* and all holdings in *cash management trusts*.

Broker An agent who handles investors' orders to buy and sell securities, commodities, insurance policies or other property. For this service, a commission is charged which, depending upon the broker and the amount of the transaction, may or may not be negotiated.

Brokerage A fee charged by a broker for the execution of a transaction; or alternatively an amount per transaction or a percentage of the total value of the transaction. Sometimes also referred to as a *commission* or fee.

Building Society A type of *non-bank financial institution,* established principally for the purposes of providing bank-type savings vehicles and home finance to individual borrowers. Building societies are regulated by the *Australian Financial Institutions Commission* and individual State-based supervisory bodies.

Bull One who believes the market will rise. (Opposite of *Bear*).

Bullion Gold or silver bars or ingots assaying at least 99.95% purity.

Bull Market An advancing market. The opposite of *Bear Market*.

Bull Spread In relation to *options* transactions, any spread in which a rise in the price of the underlying asset will theoretically increase the value of the spread. (Opposite of *Bear Spread*).

Bundesbank   The *central bank* of Germany. Established in 1957, the Bundesbank was modelled after the US *Federal Reserve*. It comprises 11 Länder or regional banks, governed by the Bundesbank Central Committee, which meets every two weeks to make decisions on foreign exchange and changes to *Lombard* and *discount rates*.

Bundled   Referring to the incorporation of a number of services or features into a single product. For example, a bundled superannuation contract might combine the various activities of investment management, insurance, trusteeship and administration into a single service; whereas an *unbundled* arrangement would see these activities being conducted by a range of different parties.

Buoyant Market   A market in which prices have a tendency to rise easily with a considerable show of strength.

Business Cycle   An irregular but recurring period of indeterminate scope and origin embracing expansion, prosperity, recession, and recovery. (See also *Economic Clock*).

Business Rules   Rules governing the procedures, rights and obligations of members of the *Australian Stock Exchange* in trading and dealing with each other and their clients. The rules are binding on the members and if the members do not obey the rules they can be suspended or expelled.

Butterfly   Referring to the sale (purchase) of two identical *options,* together with the purchase (sale) of one option with an immediately higher exercise price, and one option with an immediately lower exercise price. All options must be of the same type, have the same underlying asset and expire at the same time. (See also *Condor*).

Buy a Contract   To enter into a *futures* or *options* contract to buy a specified commodity.

Buy-back   a) In relation to managed funds or *prescribed interests,* a requirement on the investment manager to repurchase units from unitholders seeking to redeem part or all of their investment, even in cases where redemptions cannot be met by liquidating the assets of the fund; b) In relation to *derivative* markets, an offsetting purchase to 'cover' or liquidate a short sale.

Buyer's Market   A condition of the market in which there is an abundance of goods available and hence buyers can afford to be selective and may be able to buy at a lower price than had previously prevailed. (Opposite of *Seller's Market*).

Buying Hedge   The purchase of *futures contracts* to protect against the possibility that commodities or financial instruments which will be needed in the future will increase in cost.

Buy Order   An order given to a broker or a bank authorising the purchase of a specified quantity of securities or commodities.

Buy/Sell Differential   The difference between the buying and selling price of a security. (See also *Spread*).

Call Option   An *option* which gives its holder the right but not the obligation to purchase an asset at a predetermined date *(maturity date)* for a predetermined price *(exercise price)*. (See also *Put Option*).

Cap   A ceiling or maximum rate of interest under a loan. A 'capped rate loan' means that the borrower cannot pay more (but can still pay less) than the specified maximum rate of interest. (See also *Collar*).

Capital Account   The part of Australia's *Balance of Payments* relating to investment flows (ie. share and bond transactions, loans and borrowings, and the level of international reserves held by the Reserve Bank), as opposed to *current account* items such as imports and exports.

Capital Adequacy   a) An internationally-adopted standard for the prudential supervision of banks, under which minimum levels of shareholders' equity (weighted according to the risks associated with different kinds of activity) must be maintained to support the investment and lending activities of banks. (See also *Risk Weighting*); b) In relation to *public offer funds*, a requirement under the *SIS Legislation* that the *approved trustee* maintain a prescribed level of capital in cases where the trustee intends to keep custody of the fund's assets (or, alternatively, that the *custodian* is appropriately capitalised in cases where an external custodian is used).

Capital Asset Pricing Model (CAPM) A model for describing the way prices of individual assets are determined in an efficient market, based on their relative riskiness in comparison with the return on *risk-free assets*. According to this model, prices are determined in such a way that *risk premiums* are proportional to *systematic risk* as measured by the *beta* coefficient. As such, the CAPM provides an explicit expression of the expected returns for all assets. Basically, the CAPM holds that if investors are risk averse, high-risk stocks must have higher expected returns than low-risk stocks.

Capital Gain/Loss The difference between the sale price of a capital asset and its cost.

Capital Gains Tax A tax on the increase in the capital value of investments, payable when the capital gain is realised. Capital gains tax is indexed so that nominal increases in value due to inflation are not taxed as well. The taxation regime also allows *capital losses* to be offset against other taxation liabilities (eg. income tax) in certain circumstances. Most *pooled superannuation trusts* accrue either fully or in part the liability for capital gains tax on the assets held even though those gains may not yet be realised.

Capital Growth Appreciation in the capital or market value of an investment, as opposed to income which may be received from the investment from time to time, eg. dividends in the case of share investments.

Capital Guaranteed Referring to an investment product, normally offered by a *life insurance company,* which includes some form of guaranteed return of capital. The nature of the guarantee varies in format but is, typically, a 'promise to pay' by the life insurance company itself, ie. there is no external guarantor. Interest earnings are not generally guaranteed in advance. (See also *Capital Protected, Capital Stable*).

Capital-Indexed Bonds (CIBs) A form of *indexed bonds* whose proceeds on maturity are linked to movements in the *Consumer Price Index*, and which pay a small *coupon* rate eg. 1% per quarter of the variable final amount. (See also *Indexed Annuity Bonds*).

Capitalisation The sum of the total amount of various securities issued by a corporation, multiplied by the price of those securities. Capitalisation may include *bonds, debentures, preference shares* and *ordinary shares*. Similarly, the capitalisation of the share market is the sum of the value of listed shares. (See also *Market Capitalisation*).

Capital Market Line The line used in the *Capital Asset Pricing Model* to illustrate the rates of return for *efficient portfolios* depending on the risk free rate of return and the level of risk *(beta)* for a particular portfolio.

Capital Markets The markets for medium to long term investments, ie. 3 years and over, in securities such as shares and bonds, as distinct from the (shorter term) *money market*.

Capital Protected   Referring to a type of investment portfolio which is managed in such a way as to reduce or eliminate the risk of capital losses, usually through the use of quantitative techniques such as *protection overlays*. (See also *Capital Stable, Capital Guarantee* and *Protected Growth Fund*).

Capital Stable   A term usually describing unitised investment vehicles which have a high fixed interest and/or cash component. This creates a relatively stable unit price compared with *balanced* funds, which typically have a higher exposure to equity markets. Capital stable funds should also be distinguished from *capital guaranteed* funds, which in fact offer a (usually retrospective) promised return to the investor, and from *capital protected,* which aim to produce a certain minimum return while allowing a controlled participation in the expected higher gains from *growth assets.*

Capital Stock   All shares representing ownership of a business, including *preference* and *ordinary shares.*

CAPM   Abbreviation for *Capital Asset Pricing Model.*

Carded Rates   Currency exchange rates quoted by banks each day and usually listed on a daily exchange rate sheet. Carded rates usually apply to small foreign exchange transactions.

Carrying Charge   The expense, such as storage charges, insurance, interest, and other incidental costs involved in ownership of stored physical commodities over a period of time. The carrying charge may be reflected in *futures contracts* based on the physical commodities in question by successively higher prices for each succeeding future month of the contract.

CASAC   Abbreviation for *Companies and Securities Advisory Committee*.

Cash   a) Generally, coin and note currency of a country in circulation and deposited in cheque accounts and other deposits that are available upon short notice; b) One of the *asset classes* invested in as part of a typical balanced investment portfolio.

Cash and Carry   The practice which involves the purchase of a physical commodity against the forward sale of that commodity on the *futures* market.

Cash-Back Pension   Another term for *Allocated Pension*.

Cash Commodity   The actual physical commodity as distinguished from *futures contracts* based on that commodity. Also called **Spot Commodity**.

Cash Dividend   A dividend paid on a security in cash or by cheque.

Cash Equivalents   Short-term investments held in lieu of cash and readily converted into cash within a short time span (ie. *Bank Bills, Treasury Notes*, etc), generally with maturities of no longer than 180 days. Often referred to, along with cash, as *liquid assets*.

Cash Flow   In relation to company accounts, reported net income plus amounts charged off for *depreciation, amortisation*, and extraordinary charges to reserves, which are book-keeping deductions and not paid out in actual dollars and cents.

Cash Management Trust (CMT) A pooled investment vehicle for investors who would not individually have access to the professional money market. By pooling funds from various sources, larger volumes of higher yielding short-dated securities can be purchased and the resulting higher returns can then be returned to the trust members. CMTs generally restrict themselves to negotiable instruments of a duration of no longer than six months. As these securities are highly liquid, a CMT can accommodate cash flows, both in and out, on a daily basis, thereby offering small investors a flexibility not present in a traditional fixed rate term deposit.

Cash Settlement The settlement on some *options* and *futures* contracts that do not require delivery of the underlying security. For options, the difference between the *settlement price* on the underlying asset and the option's *exercise price* is paid to the option holder at exercise. For futures contracts, the exchange establishes a settlement price on the final day of trading and all remaining open positions are marked to market at that price.

CD Abbreviation for *Certificate of Deposit*.

CEDA Abbreviation for *Committee for the Economic Development of Australia*.

Central Bank Also known as a **government bank**. A country's central bank is generally the authority responsible for regulating its monetary and banking systems and currency note supply. Although central banks do not dictate interest and exchange rates per se, the actions they take in foreign exchange and domestic fixed interest markets, particularly in the sale and purchase of government bonds, have a profound effect on financial markets. An interventionist central bank may impose controls on foreign exchange and lending or ceilings on interest rates. (See also *Bank of England*, *Bundesbank*, *Federal Reserve*, and *Reserve Bank of Australia*).

Certificate The actual piece of paper which is evidence of ownership (eg. of shares in a corporation).

Certificate of Deposit (CD) A written certificate by a bank or financial institution stating that a fixed dollar amount has been deposited with it for a fixed period of time at a predetermined rate of interest.

CGIS Abbreviation for **Commonwealth Government Inscribed Stock**, the main type of bond issued by the Commonwealth of Australia.

Charting The graphing of market variables – particularly prices, averages and trading volume – in order to ascertain trends and to project future values. (See also *Technical Analysis*).

CHESS Abbreviation for *Clearing House Electronic Subregister System*.

Chinese Wall An imaginary 'wall' comprising procedures and policies adopted to avoid conflicts of interest within an organisation (eg. to separate the sharebroking and investment management operations of a financial services group).

Churning The practice of acquiring a holding of shares and then placing both buying and selling orders for those shares (usually at about the same price or slightly higher) in order to build up turnover.

CIR Abbreviation for *Collective Investment Review*.

CIS Abbreviation for *Collective Investment Scheme*.

Civil Penalty Order An order issued by a Court, on application of the Insurance and Superannuation Commissioner or his delegate, that a person has contravened *a civil penalty provision* under the *SIS Legislation*. The order may include a substantial fine if the Court considers the breach to have been a serious one.

Civil Penalty Provisions Provisions in the *SIS Legislation*, the contravention of which involves civil or (where the contravention is found to have been intentional, reckless or dishonest) criminal sanctions.

Clearing House A department within an exchange or an independent corporation through which all trades on a particular exchange must be confirmed, matched and settled.

Clearing House Electronic Subregister System (CHESS) An electronic transfer and settlement system introduced by the Australian Stock Exchange in 1995 to replace the *Flexible Accelerated Securities Transfer* (FAST) system. CHESS replaces physical transfer documents in the share settlement process. It automatically issues updated holdings statements to the investor, and details of all shareholdings on its register to the stock issuer.

Clearing Member A firm qualified to clear trades through a *clearing house* or clearing corporation.

Clearing System An institutional arrangement for transferring securities and payments between sellers and buyers subsequent to the establishment of a trading price.

Closed-end Fund A pooled fund which no longer accepts new investors or (sometimes) new investments from existing unitholders. These are usually difficult funds for investors to exit owing to a lack of liquidity in the fund's underlying investments. (Opposite of *Open-end Fund*).

Closing Price The price at which the final transaction in a security took place on a particular business day. Share prices are quoted daily in the financial pages of leading newspapers and show opening, high, low and last sale (closing) prices, plus net change from the previous day.

Closing Transaction A transaction in which the seller (writer) of an *option* terminates his/her obligation. In the case of a listed option, a seller effects a closing transaction by purchasing a new listed option having the same terms as the option which is being sold.

CMSF Abbreviation for *Conference of Major Superannuation Funds*.

CMT Abbreviation for *Cash Management Trust*.

Codification The translation of common law legal principles and precedents into statute law. The duties of superannuation fund trustees spelt out in the *SIS Legislation* are an example of codification, drawing upon decades of judicial decisions and refinements of common law principles of trust.

Collar Referring to a loan facility in which both maximum and minimum interest rates are specified. The maximum rate acts as a *cap*, while the minimum rate is a *floor* below which the interest rate will not be allowed to fall.

Collateral Securities or other property pledged by a borrower to secure payment of a loan.

Collective Investment A generic term for investment products such as *unit trusts* which are managed by professional managers on behalf of numerous individual investors. The term 'collective investments' covers a wide variety of investment schemes, with the clearest common characteristic being the involvement of a professional manger who manages the total fund or collection of assets to produce a return which is shared by all investors. A common form of collective investment is a unit trust, but there are numerous other types (eg. racehorse syndicates, agricultural plantation schemes). Most are subject to regulation under the *Corporations Law* and will be subject to the proposed *Collective Investments Review* legislation when it takes effect. (See also *Commingled Fund* and *Pooled Investment*).

Collective Investment Review (CIR) A review of the regulatory structure of Australia's *collective investment* industry, undertaken by the *Australian Law Reform Commission* and *Companies and Securities Advisory Committee* in 1992-94. At the time of going to print (April 1996), the CIR had progressed to the point of draft legislation, planned to be introduced to the Commonwealth Parliament during 1996. One of the main features of the proposed legislation is the replacement of the dual roles of manager and trustee of collective investment schemes by a single responsible entity or *scheme operator*.

Collective Investment Scheme (CIS) A *unit trust* or pooled investment vehicle under the *Collective Investment Review* legislation.

Commercial Paper Negotiable, short-term, unsecured *promissory notes* issued in bearer form, usually on a discount basis, by a corporation to raise working capital for any term normally up to 180 days.

Commercial Property Property intended for use or occupancy by retail and wholesale businesses (eg. stores, office buildings, hotels and service establishments).

Commingled Fund The *collective investment* of the assets of a number of small funds, sometimes through a *master fund* arrangement, allowing for broader and more efficient investing.

Commission The broker's basic fee for purchasing or selling securities (or property) as an agent. This fee is generally negotiated. Also known as **Brokerage**.

Committee for the Economic Development of Australia (CEDA) An independent association established in 1960 to promote discussion, objective research and inter-disciplinary communication in the interests of development of the national economy and of the future of Australia. CEDA draws its membership from the business, professional and academic communities, and has offices in all mainland capitals and the ACT.

Commodity A tradeable item that can generally be further processed and sold; including industrial (metals), agricultural (wool, wheat, sugar, etc) and bulk (coal, iron ore) goods. Commodities are important to the Australian economy as they account for the majority of our exports.

Common Factor An economic or other factor which affects the return on virtually all securities.

Commutation In relation to superannuation benefits, the process of converting a *pension* or *annuity* into a lump sum.

Companies and Securities Advisory Committee (CASAC) A Committee established under the *Corporations Law* to advise the Commonwealth Attorney-General on proposals for corporate law reform and improvements to the efficiency of the Australian securities and futures markets. Along with the *Australian Law Reform Commission,* CASAC was responsible for a major review of collective investments schemes in 1992-94, leading to a number of expected legislative changes to that sector during 1996. (See also *Collective Investment Review*).

Companies Auditors and Liquidators Disciplinary Board
A Board established under the *Corporations Law* to determine whether auditors or liquidators have failed to properly perform their duties. Penalties which the Board may impose include cancellation or suspension of the individual's licence, imposition of restrictions on conduct or an admonition.

Company A legal entity regulated by the *Australian Securities Commission* under the *Corporations Law*. Also referred to as a *Corporation*. Companies can take a number of different forms, including: a) a **company limited by shares,** where shareholders' liability is limited to the amount of unpaid shares; b) a **company limited by guarantee,** where liability is limited to an amount prescribed in the company's memorandum of association; c) a **no-liability company** (restricted to mining companies only); and d) a **proprietary limited** (or **private**) **company,** where shareholding is restricted to a small number of shareholders and restrictions are placed on transfers of shares.

Compliance Procedures undertaken at regular intervals or on an on-going basis to ensure internal and external controls and regulations are complied with.

Complying Fund A superannuation fund which complies with the operational standards specified in the *SIS Regulations* and is thereby eligible to receive concessional taxation treatment. (See also *Regulated Superannuation Fund*).

Compounding   The arithmetical process of determining the final value of an investment or series of investments when *compound interest* is applied, ie. when interest is earned on the interest as well as on the initial principal. Investment returns are typically compounded, so two consecutive periods of 10% returns results in a compound return of 21%. (See also *Annualising*).

Compound Interest   A method of interest calculation where, in each period, interest is calculated on both the principal and interest previously accrued. Henry Ford once said that compound interest was 'the eighth wonder of the world'. (Opposite of *Simple Interest*).

Compound Option   An *option* instrument that gives the holder the right, but not the obligation, to buy another specified option prior to a given expiry date.

Compulsory Superannuation   A policy adopted by the Hawke and Keating Labor Governments, requiring contributions to superannuation funds by or on behalf of virtually all employed Australians. (See also *Superannuation Guarantee Charge*).

Condor   Referring to the sale (purchase) of two *options* with consecutive *exercise prices,* together with the purchase (sale) of one option with an immediately lower exercise price and one option with an immediately higher exercise price. All options must be of the same type, have the same underlying asset, and expire at the same time. (See also *Butterfly*).

Conference of Major Superannuation Funds (CMSF)   A major annual forum for superannuation fund trustees, managers and service providers, with a particular focus on issues facing industry funds. The CMSF is the keynote annual event for the *Australian Institute of Superannuation Trustees*.

Confirmation Note   A written document confirming a transaction struck between two dealers or between a broker and a client. Alternatively referred to as a **Contract Note**.

Conglomerate   A corporation that has diversified its operations, usually by acquiring enterprises in widely varied industries.

Consideration   The 'price' for which the promises of another is bought when entering into a contract. Consideration may take the form of a right, interest, profit or benefit accruing to one party or some forbearance, detriment, loss or responsibility given, suffered or undertaken by the other.

Constant Proportion Portfolio Insurance (CPPI)   A risk management technique of *dynamic hedging*. 'Constant proportion' refers to the fact that the portfolio constantly maintains a cushion of cash large enough to ensure no negative return to the end of a defined protection period, even in the event of a sudden crash. This 'cushion' or percentage weighting to cash versus growth assets will fluctuate throughout the risk cycle, depending on current interest rate levels.

Constitutional Corporation A term used in the *SIS Legislation* to describe the legal status a superannuation fund must have if it wishes to meet one of two alternative criteria to be a *Regulated Superannuation Fund* and thereby be eligible for concessional taxation treatment. The alternative method is that the fund has, as its main purpose, the provision of age pensions. (See also *Corporate Trustee*).

Consumer Price Index (CPI) An index measuring the prices at various times of a selected group of goods and services which typify those bought by ordinary Australian households. It allows comparisons of the relative cost of living over time, and is used as a measure of inflation. (See also *Average Weekly Earnings*).

Consumer Price Index 1980 -1995

per cent 14
12
10
8
6
4
2

80 81 82 83 84 85 86 87 88 89 90 91 92 93 94 95

Consumption Tax See *Goods and Services Tax*.

Contango A relationship in which spot or cash prices are lower than futures (or forward) prices. (Opposite of *Backwardation*).

Contingent Liability A liability or obligation which may arise in the event of a certain occurence; eg. the damages which might have to be paid to an external party in the event of a successful legal action. Contingent liabilities are not taken into account in the company's balance sheet. Rather, they are normally disclosed in notes to the company's accounts.

Continuous Disclosure A regulatory requirement under the *Corporations Law* for companies, listed entities and prescribed interest schemes to disclose to the ASC for public release any "material matter" which is likely to affect their financial position or credit standing, or which investors would reasonably require to know in order to be able to make an informed investment decision. Continuous disclosure is an additional obligation to prospectus disclosure and periodic financial returns. It was introduced by the Commonwealth's Corporate Law Reform Act 1994, and will extend to many products in Australia's superannuation industry through the incorporation of parallel provisions into the *SIS Legislation*.

Continuous Market A market in which transactions occur whenever selling orders are matched or exceeded by buying orders. The Stock Exchange is an example of a continuous market.

Contract An agreement between individuals, companies or other entities which binds each party and is legally enforceable. Contracts are used in many facets of business and investment markets, including areas such as employment, engagement of investment managers and service providers, and transactions of securities. (See also *Futures Contract, Management Agreement*).

Contract Month   The future month in which delivery or cash settlement is to be made under a *futures contract*.

Contract Note   See *Confirmation Note*.

Contrarian Investor   An investor who invests against market trends, as opposed to following the prevailing consensus view.

Contribution   An amount of money placed into a fund. In relation to superannuation funds, contributions may be made by either employers or employees or both.

Contribution Holiday   A period of time over which the sponsor of a *defined benefit fund* is not required to make contributions to the plan owing to an actuarial assessment that current assets and reserves are sufficient to meet the plan's liabilities for the time being.

Contributions Tax   The 15% tax levied on certain contributions to superannuation funds.

Convergence   The tendency of *futures* and cash prices to come together as the delivery month approaches.

Conversion   In relation to options markets, long underlying position together with a short call and long put, where both options have the same exercise price and expiration date. A conversion is a long underlying position offset by a synthetic short underlying position.

Convertible Notes   Securities which are convertible into the ordinary shares of a company at a prescribed price or ratio at specified times at the option of the holder. Convertible *Bonds* and *Debentures* may also be issued by corporations or government bodies. Convertible Notes are attractive to some investors in that they may display certain properties of both shares and fixed interest securities.

Convexity   The sensitivity of the *duration* of a bond to changing interest rates. A high convexity means that the price of the bond in question will be more responsive to interest rate fluctuations.

Conveyance   The means by which title to real estate is transferred.

Core Portfolio   A portfolio comprising (generally) the bulk of a fund's assets, which is invested in a highly controlled fashion in an attempt to secure the fund's liabilities with a reasonable degree of confidence. The balance of the fund's assets may then be managed more aggressively in search of higher than average returns. (See also *Active Management*).

Corporate Bond   An instrument written under seal whereby a company acknowledges that a stated sum is owed, which it will repay at a specified date. The company is also obliged to pay a stipulated amount of interest to the bondholders.

Corporate Governance   A generic term covering issues associated with the management practices, Board structures and personnel policies of companies. From the investor's point of view, corporate governance is normally concerned with the degree of influence which should be exerted over companies by their shareholders in order to advance their financial interests, normally though the exercise of voting rights or proxies at the companies' Annual General Meetings. Corporate governance is becoming an increasingly significant issue in Australia's superannuation and fund management industries, as the volume of institutional investment increases and attention is focused on the proper exercise of trustees' and managers' *fiduciary* responsibilities.

Corporate Trustee   A superannuation fund trustee which has been incorporated as a company. Incorporation of a trustee board may occur to meet the *Constitutional Corporation* provisions of the SIS legislation. Alternatively, it may exist because the trustee is a professional Public Trustee Company or the employer-sponsor of the fund has established a special company to take on the responsibility of trusteeship. Individuals appointed to exercise fiduciary responsibilities in corporate trustees are called *Trustee Directors*.

Corporation   Another term for *company*. The term is also sometimes used to refer to public sector enterprises which engage in business activities.

Corporations Law   A series of Acts of the Australian Parliament regulating companies and the securities and futures industries in Australia. The Corporations Law is administered by the *Australian Securities Commission (ASC)*.

Corporations Power The Commonwealth Government's power under section 51(xx) of the Australian Constitution which authorises it to regulate and control the activities of "trading and financial corporations". The Corporations power is the legal foundation of the *Corporations Law* and (in conjunction with the *Pensions Power*) of the rules governing superannuation fund trustees under the *SIS Legislation*. (See also *Constitutional Corporation*).

Corporatisation The alteration of the reporting, legal and management structure of a public trading body to allow it to operate at arm's length from the Government, with profit as a major objective. Unlike privatised bodies, corporatised bodies remain under government ownership and control and are not usually subject to the *Corporations Law*. (See also *privatisation*).

Correction A movement in prices which reverses a previous trend. The term is normally used to refer to a lowering of share prices after a sustained period of increase.

Correspondent Bank A bank that, in its own country, handles the banking for banks from another country.

Council of Financial Supervisors A coordinating body established in 1992 which brings together Australia's main financial supervisory authorities. The Council is chaired by the *Reserve Bank of Australia*. Its other members are the *Insurance and Superannuation Commission, Australian Securities Commission* and *Australian Financial Institutions Commission*.

Counter-Cyclical Referring to an investment style which aims to anticipate and take advantage of expected turns in the *business cycle;* eg. to sell out of equity investments after a prolonged period of growth in anticipation of a cyclical dip or recession.

Counterparty The customer or bank with whom a foreign exchange or *over-the-counter options* deal is made. The term is also used in interest and currency swaps markets to refer to a participant in a *swap* exchange.

Counterparty Risk The risk that the other party to a contract will not fulfil the terms of the contract.

Coupon A certificate attached to a bond, representing an obligation to pay interest on the bond. Not to be confused with the *yield*, which varies as interest rates move. (See also *Zero Coupon Bonds*).

Coupon Payments The periodic interest payments on a bond.

Coupon Rate The annual value of a bond's coupon payments, expressed as a percentage of the bond's *par value*.

Covariance A measure of the degree to which two variables move in relation to each other. A positive covariance means that both variables tend to be above or below their *mean* at the same time.

Covenant An agreement or promise, under which one party pledges to the other that something has been done or will be done, or vouches for the truth of certain facts. Covenants are either positive or negative, and relate as a rule to the relationship between vendor and purchaser, or landlord and tenant. A positive covenant is one by which the party binds him/herself to do some act or carry his/her rights in relation to the other party, or promises not to do a certain thing. Covenants are also express or implied: express, where they are set out in terms; implied, where the mere relationship of the parties automatically creates the covenant.

Cover To close out a position previously taken, for example, by taking a *long position* equal to an existing *short position*.

Covered Call A *call option* whose seller (writer) owns the underlying security and is able to deliver it if the option is exercised.

Covered Put A *put option* whose seller (writer) owns a put on the same underlying security with an *exercise price* equal to or greater than the exercise price of the put written, or who has sold the underlying security short.

Covered Write The sale of a *call option* against an existing long position in the underlying security.

CPA Abbreviation for **Certified Practising Accountant**, a member of the *Australian Society of Certified Practising Accountants*.

CPI Abbreviation for *Consumer Price Index*.

CPPI Abbreviation for *Constant Proportion Portfolio Insurance*.

CRB Index Abbreviation for **Commodities Research Bureau Index,** a United States Index of global commodity prices.

Credit Foncier Loan A loan which is repaid in instalments comprising both principal and interest components. Most mortgages are structured this way. (See also *Amortisation*).

Crediting Rate In relation to superannuation, the rate at which fund earnings are attributed to members' accounts. The crediting rate may differ from the fund's actual *earnings rate;* eg. if the trustees have adopted a *smoothing* policy in relation to their year-to-year investment returns.

Credit Rating The financial standing of a company, government or financial institution relative to others. The credit rating determines what the institution will be charged to raise funds, in relation both to the amount it is able to raise and the interest it will be charged. (See also *Australian Ratings, Moody's, Standard & Poors*).

Credit Risk The risk of suffering loss due to another party defaulting on its financial obligations.

Credit Union A type of *non-bank financial institution* for personal savings and loans, structured on a co-operative basis. Historically, credit unions were established on the basis of a common bond among their membership, eg. workplace, local community, and existed to provide savings and personal loan facilities to their members. Many have now diversified their activities and grown into significant institutions within their respective localities or States. Regulated by the *Australian Financial Institutions Commission* and individual State-based supervisory bodies.

Crossing The buying and selling of *futures contracts* simultaneously in the same contract month for the same commodity. A broker may do this where he has orders both to buy and to sell; strict exchange rules apply to the practice.

Cross Hedging The practice of hedging currency on the basis of a foreign *cross rate* (eg. US dollar vs. Japanese yen), rather than the local *exchange rate* (eg. Australian dollar vs. US dollar).

Cross Rate An exchange rate between two currencies, usually constructed from the individual exchange rates of the two currencies, measured against the United States dollar.

Cross Subsidisation The use of revenue generated in one area of a business to supplement returns or prevent losses in another.

Cum Dividend Referring to a share or unit in a *unit trust* which is trading such that buyers rather than sellers qualify to receive the next dividend payment. This is usually reflected in the price of the security in question. (Opposite of *Ex-Dividend*).

Cum Rights A share which is trading such that buyers receive the right to a new issue, usually resulting in a higher price. (Opposite of *Ex Rights*).

Cumulative Rate of Return A rate of return covering (generally) more than one year. If a fund earns 15% in the first year, 36% in the second year and -7% in the third year, its cumulative return is 45.45%. Its annual average *compound* return, by comparison, is 13.3%. It is always advisable to look at the individual annual returns which make up cumulative and compound returns in making judgements about the quality and consistency of returns.

Currency A country's unit of exchange that has a value in terms of purchasing goods and services within a country and in purchasing units of other countries' currencies. However, some currencies are not convertible into the value of other currencies.

Currency Basket Option See *Basket Option*.

Currency Forward A *forward contract* where the commodity to be exchanged, at the predetermined amount and date as agreed by two parties, is currency.

Currency Option An *option* contract which gives the buyer the right (but not the obligation) to buy or sell a specified amount of a foreign currency in exchange for another on or before a specified future date. Sometimes used to *hedge* securities held in overseas markets. Also known as **FX Option.**

Currency Overlay An investment management technique aimed at protecting an investor's overseas currency exposure by means of a *dynamic hedging* model.

Currency Risk Risk of incurring losses in relation to the value of overseas investments as a result of movements in international exchange rates.

Currency Swap See *Swap*.

Current Account The part of Australia's *Balance of Payments* relating to imports and exports of goods and services and the net effect of income received and payments made on Australia's foreign debt and investments. A **Current Account Deficit** means that the sum of all these activities yields a negative figure. (See also *Capital Account*).

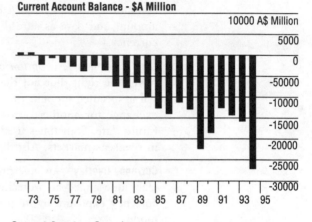

Current Account Balance - $A Million

Current Assets See *Assets*.

Current Prices The most recent sale prices prevailing in the market at a specific moment of time.

Current Yield Annual *interest, coupon* or *dividend* divided by market price per bond or share to determine the income return, expressed as a *yield* based on the current market price. (See also *Running Yield*).

Custodian An organisation which safeguards and maintains assets (eg. cash, securities) on behalf of other people. Unlike a *trustee,* a custodian is solely responsible for holding assets on behalf of others; it does not strictly own the assets on behalf of beneficiaries (or unitholders in the case of a unit trust), and is not subject to the same fiduciary duties as trustees. Trustee companies generally also act as custodians, as do many banks. Those custodians who aggregate a series of portfolios are known as **Master Custodians,** usually managed by different investment managers, in order to provide a single overall report on the fund. By contrast, a custodian who holds assets on behalf of clients in a number of different countries is known as a **Global Custodian.** (See also *Trustee*).

Custody Possession of securities by a financial institution on behalf of others, for purposes of safekeeping. (See also *Custodian*).

Cutting a Loss The decision to close out an unprofitable market position and take the loss involved before it becomes larger.

Cyclical Stocks Shares which move directly with the *business cycle*; generally they advance as business conditions improve and decline when business slackens. Mining companies are typically cyclical, and the shares of Australian banks and media companies have been shown to be very sensitive to domestic conditions.

D_{AA}

DAA   See *Development Allowance Authority*

Day Order   An order to a broker to buy or sell shares only on the day when the order is entered.

Dealer   An individual who places orders to buy or sell securities.

Dealer's Licence   A licence issued by the *Australian Securities Commission* under the *Corporations Law* to a person in the business of dealing in debentures, shares, prescribed interests and options. The licence will invariably be subject to conditions, including liquidity requirements.

Debenture   A type of *debt security* backed by the general credit of the issuer and not by a specific security.

Debt-Equity Mix   In relation to investment portfolios, the relativities between cash/fixed interest and *growth assets* held within the overall portfolio. For example, a growth-oriented portfolio might have a debt-equity mix of 25% debt and 75% equity, while for a more conservative capital stable portfolio the mix might be 70%:30% in favour of cash and fixed interest.

Debt Ratio   The extent to which a company's total assets are financed with borrowed funds (ie. borrowings divided by total assets). An important financial statistic.

Debt Security   A security representing borrowed funds that must be repaid by the issuer (eg. *bonds, certificates of deposit, debentures*). If the Government issues bonds, it is borrowing funds. Purchasers of the bonds are thus lenders to the Government.

Debt to Equity Ratio   The relationship between funds provided by creditors and funds provided by shareholders (ie. borrowings divided by shareholders' funds).

Decile   A statistical measure dividing a sample into ten numerically equal groups. (See also *Percentile* and *Quartile*).

Deductible   Referring to expenses which can be offset against taxation liabilities. Certain contributions to superannuation funds, for example, are tax deductible up to prescribed limits.

Default   Failure to perform a contractual obligation.

Default Premium   The difference between the promised yield on a bond and that which is actually expected in light of the possibility that the issuer of the bond might default on its obligation.

Defeasance   An arrangement under which a borrower's obligation to creditors is passed on to a third party. For example a bank, in exchange for a fee, might undertake to assume a company's obligation to make principal and interest payments to the company's *debenture* holders.

Deferred Annuity   A type of *annuity* which commences payment of income at a later date. *Eligible termination payments* can be 'rolled-over' into deferred annuities, in which case a pension will be required to commence on or before the purchaser's 65th birthday. (See also *Allocated Pension* and *Approved Deposit Fund*).

Deferred Delivery   The trading of shares even though the owner in some circumstances may not yet have the certificates.

Deficit   An excess of expenditure over income or revenue. (Opposite of *Surplus*).

Defined Benefit Fund   A superannuation fund in which the benefits to be paid to the member are defined in advance of the member's retirement. The benefit is usually expressed as a proportion (eg. two-thirds, or 75%, etc) of the member's salary on retirement. In these funds it is generally the company or sponsor of the fund (rather than the member) which carries the risk as to the ability of the fund to meet its liabilities. (Opposite of *Defined Contribution Fund*, or *Accumulation Fund*).

Defined Contribution Fund   A superannuation fund in which the amount of contribution payable (as distinct from the end benefit) is defined (eg. 10% of salary). In these funds, the benefit payable to a member on retirement constitutes the aggregate of contributions to the fund (both employer and employee) in respect of the member, plus the investment earnings on those contributions. Unlike a *defined benefit fund*, the investment risk in a defined contribution fund is borne by the fund members. (Also known as **Accumulation Fund**).

Deflation   A general price decline during which consumer spending is substantially curtailed, bank loans contract and the amount of money in circulation is reduced. It is the opposite of *inflation* and generally applies to more than just a temporary decline. The early 1990s saw some evidence of deflation, particularly in financial asset and property prices.

Delisting   The removal of a company's shares from listing on the stock exchange. This may occur because the company has failed to comply with the exchange's rules, or no longer meets listing requirements (eg. has been taken over).

Deliverable Types   The actual types or grades of physical commodity which may be delivered under *Sydney Futures Exchange* rules in settlement of a *futures contract.*

Delivery   The transfer of possession of securities from one individual or firm to another in fulfilment of contracts made on an exchange and on terms which meet all of the requirements of that exchange.

Delivery Month   In the futures market, the calendar month during which delivery can be made or taken on a *futures contract.*

Delivery Points   Locations designated by futures exchanges at which the physical commodity covered by a *futures contract* may be delivered in fulfilment of such a contract.

Delta   The expected expansion or contraction in an *option premium* given a small change in the value of the underlying security. *Call options* have positive deltas; *put options* have negative deltas. The delta may change as the option gets closer to its expiry.

Delta Hedging   A method of hedging exposures to option markets by purchasing or selling the underlying securities in proportion to the option's *delta.*

Depreciation   The writing-down of the cost of an asset systematically over the life of that asset.

Depression   A prolonged slump in economic activity, characterised by rising unemployment and serious falls in production and consumption of goods. (See also *Recession*).

Derivative   A financial contract that derives its value from an *underlying security*, liability or index. Derivatives come in many varieties, including *forwards*, *futures*, *options*, *share ratios*, *warrants* and *swaps*. Also known as **synthetic**.

Develop Australia Bonds   See *Infrastructure Bonds*.

Development Allowance Authority (DAA)   The Commonwealth Government authority responsible for the approval, management and monitoring of functions relating to *infrastructure bonds*. The DAA was originally established to administer depreciation allowances for qualifying development projects, and was given its current expanded responsibilities in 1994 when the Federal Government passed legislation defining the eligibility criteria for infrastructure bonds and providing significant taxation concessions for investment in them. Also known as **Invest Australia**, which is its trading name.

Development Capital   Can have a variety of meanings, but usually refers to investments in relatively small, unlisted companies which have an established track record in their field of business, and which require new funding to finance their expansion. This contrasts with *venture capital*, which in Australian usage tends to refer to investments in start-up companies only. Certain aspects of the development capital sector are sometimes referred to as *private equity* or patient capital. (See also *Leveraged Buy-Out, Management Buy-Out, Mezzanine Finance* and *Private Equity*).

Discounting

Director   A person elected by shareholders to be responsible for the management and operation of the company. Executive directors are directly involved in the operation of the business, whereas non-executive directors are not involved in the day to day operations of the company and may only be on the Board.

Direct Property   Investments held directly in real estate, as opposed to 'indirect' property investments such as units in a *property trust*.

Direct Quotation   An exchange rate quotation in which the local currency is the term currency and the foreign currency is the base currency (eg. a direct quotation USD/DEM 1.7162). (See also *Indirect Quotation*).

Disclaimer   A statement which may allow a person or corporation to avoid liability, if before or at the time of giving advice, that person or corporation makes it clear that he or she accepts no responsibility for his or her statement. Disclaimers are often found in disclosure documents (eg. prospectuses for *collective investment* products), to the effect that the manager of the product does not guarantee the level of performance of the fund or the return of capital to investors.

Discount   a) The difference between the original offering price of a security and the price to which it may fall in the 'after offering' market; b) The amount by which a security sells below its asset backing. The opposite of *Premium*; c) The *present value* of a specified sum of money to be received in a specified number of years.

Discounting   The process of calculating the *present value* of a stream of future cash flows.

Discount Rate   The *discount* expressed as a rate per cent per annum related to the face value of a *bank bill* or *promissory note*. (See also *Yield*).

Discretionary Account   A trading account over which an investor gives a broker authority to effect transactions without prior reference to or approval of that client.

Discretionary Fund   See *Master Fund*.

Disqualified Person   A person or organisation which is disqualified from being an investment manager of a superannuation fund under the *SIS Legislation*. The grounds for disqualification include that the individual (or employee) has been convicted of an offence in respect of dishonest conduct, or (in the case of a body corporate) is in receivership or liquidation.

Diversification   The spreading of investment funds among classes of securities and localities in order to distribute and control risk. This is a fundamental law of investment, meaning simply: 'don't put all your eggs in one basket'.

Divestment   The disposal of an asset by sale.

Dividend   The amount of a company's after-tax earnings which it pays to shareholders.

Dividend Discount Model   A model for determining the price of a security based on the discounted value of its projected future dividend payments. These models are very sensitive to interest rates.

Dividend Imputation A tax rule under which tax paid at the company level is credited to individual shareholders. Dividend imputation works by assessing shareholders on the total amount of the dividend and the *imputation credit*, and then allowing them to claim a tax rebate equal to the imputation credit. Dividend imputation affects the valuation of the sharemarket for taxable investors. (See also *Franked Dividend*).

Dividend Per Share See *Earnings per Share*.

Dividend Yield The return on share investment, calculated by dividing the *dividend* rate (in cents per share) by the market price of the share.

Dollar Bloc The group of countries whose currency denomination is the dollar, in particular Australia, Canada, New Zealand and the United States. Although these currencies do not necessarily have any more in common with each other than with other currencies, investors tend to link the strength of the American dollar to the attractiveness of other dollar currencies.

Dollar Weighted Return See *Money Weighted Rate of Return*.

Double Dipping The practice of exhausting concessionally-taxed superannuation savings (particularly *lump sums*) in a short period of time after retirement, and then claiming eligibility for the age pension. Government superannuation policy has progressively moved to diminish opportunities for double dipping through the introduction of measures which limit the size of lump sum payments and encourage benefits to be taken in the form of *annuities* rather than lump sums.

Double Ups   Derivative *options* that include rights either to buy or to sell within a set time period, at a particular price. The investment strategy is that the asset will either rise or fall, but will not remain static.

Dow Jones Index   A *share price index* measuring the market prices of 30 representative industrial companies on the New York Stock Exchange. The United States equivalent of the Australian *50 Leaders Index*. There are broader measures of the United States sharemarket, notably the *S&P500*, which more closely corresponds to Australia's *All Ordinaries Index*.

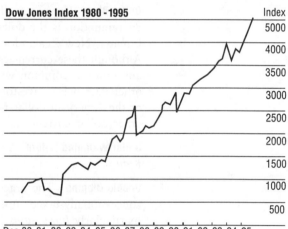

Dow Jones Index 1980 - 1995

Index: 5000, 4000, 3500, 3000, 2500, 2000, 1500, 1000, 500

Dec 80 81 82 83 84 85 86 87 88 89 90 91 92 93 94 95

Downside Protection   A *hedge* constructed to limit the adverse impact on the value of an investment of a negative movement in market or security prices.

Drawer The party who issues a *Bill of Exchange*. The drawer is liable to pay on maturity the face value of the bill to its holder, should the *acceptor* fail to pay.

Due Date The maturity date; the date when a bond, note, or other evidence of debt becomes payable or legally demandable.

Due Diligence a) The process of checking and verifying information contained in a statement to be released to the public, eg. a *prospectus*, prior to the registration of that statement; b) Ensuring that sufficient analysis has been conducted before making a loan or recommending an investment to a client.

Duration A measure of the sensitivity of fixed interest investments to changing interest rates. Duration takes into account not only the redemption date but also the dates on which interest *(coupon payments)* are paid and the amount of such interest. Duration is an important measure of the interest rate sensitivity of a fixed interest portfolio and a more sophisticated measure of the maturity of the holdings in that portfolio. (See also *Convexity*).

Dynamic Hedging A technique by which a fund's exposure to a risky asset class, eg. equities or foreign currency, is adjusted on a frequent basis, both to avoid losses where the particular asset falls in value, or to participate in the gains when it increases in value. (See also *Currency Overlay*, *Hedging*).

EAFE Index Abbreviation for **Europe, Australasia and Far East Index,** a world stock market index, often used as an ex-United States world equity benchmark by United States investors.

Earnings Before Interest and Tax (EBIT) A key measure of the financial performance of a company. It is similar to net profit, except that the effects of tax benefits, deductions and loans are factored out, yielding a truer measure of performance.

Earnings Per Share (EPS) A measure of a company's performance, calculated by dividing the company's net operating profit after tax divided by the number of shares on issue. What the investor actually receives in the hand is known as **Dividends Per Share,** which is the proportion of earnings actually paid to shareholders. (See *Payout Ratio*).

Earnings Multiple Another term for *Price-Earnings Ratio*.

Earnings Rate The rate of return on funds invested, usually expressed in terms of percent per annum.

Earnings Yield A ratio calculated by dividing a company's earnings per share by its current share price. The reciprocal of the *price-earnings ratio*.

Ease A minor and/or slow decline in the prices of a market.

EBIT Abbreviation for *Earnings Before Interest and Tax*.

Econometrics The statistical estimation of economic relationships using empirical data. These relationships are often extrapolated to provide forecasts of economic variables.

Economic Clock A model for depicting the normal sequence of events for share and property market cycles. After interest rates fall, the share market rises, followed by commodities, inflation and then property. Interest rates then rise to curb inflation and the cycle goes into decline.

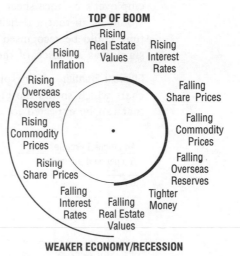

Economic Society of Australia A professional association for economists, established in 1925. The Society aims to promote discussion of economic issues and provide information and education to members.

ED53 Abbreviation for **Exposure Draft 53 – Accounting for Employee Entitlements,** a draft accounting standard which proposes that any differences between the value of accrued benefits and actual plan assets in a company-sponsored superannuation fund should be taken into account on the employer's balance sheet. Adoption of this standard would mean that a deficit in a superannuation fund could be recognised as a liability, and a surplus as an asset, of the company concerned.

Efficient Frontier A line plotted on a risk/return chart which shows the highest investment return that can be expected for any given level of risk.

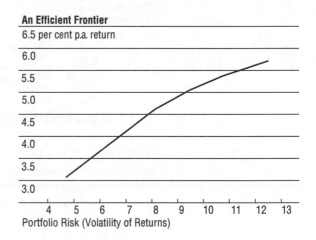

An Efficient Frontier

6.5 per cent p.a. return

Portfolio Risk (Volatility of Returns)

Efficient Market Hypothesis The assertion that 'information' cannot be used to generate superior performance since all public information on a company is immediately reflected in its share price. In such a market, an investor can attain no more, no less, than a fair return for the risks undertaken.

Efficient Portfolio   A portfolio that is fully diversified and lies on the *efficient frontier*. For any given return, no other portfolio has less risk, and for a given level of risk, no other portfolio provides superior returns.

Electronic Trade Confirmation System (ETC)   The generic term for any message or interface service that enables investors, brokers and custodians to electronically exchange confirmations that trade settlements have occurred. Although ETCs have replaced slower paper-based confirmation systems, most are incompatible. Several initiatives are currently under way to establish a global ETC, the largest being *SWIFT*.

Eligible Rollover Fund (ERF)   A type of *superannuation* fund which can accept contributions from 'protected members' who have small account balances. ERFs are required by the *SIS Legislation* to meet certain conditions regarding the reduction of account balances by fees and charges.

Eligible Service Period (ESP)   The period of time spent in the employment of a certain employer, or in membership of a certain superannuation fund, for the purposes of calculating an *Eligible Termination Payment*.

Eligible Termination Payment (ETP)   A payment made to an employee upon retirement, resignation, retrenchment or disablement, and capable of being 'rolled-over' into investments such as *Approved Deposit Funds* in order to defer and minimise taxation liability. Examples of ETPs include superannuation lump sum payments and redundancy payments. (See also *Deferred Annuity*).

Emerging Markets Financial markets in countries with developing economies, where industrialisation has commenced and the economy has linkages with the global economy. The financial markets in these countries are immature compared to those of the world's major financial centres, but are becoming increasingly sophisticated and integrated into the international markets. These markets provide potentially high returns but are subject to high risk and volatility. Current examples would include Indonesia and Mexico. (See also *Tiger Economies*).

Employee Share Acquisition Company (ESAC) A company established to operate and administer an *Employee Share Ownership Plan,* typically on the basis of subscriptions related to employees' salary bonuses or profits of the sponsoring employer.

Employee Share Ownership Plan (ESOP) A scheme established by an employer to provide tax-advantaged share ownership for its employees as part of their remuneration packages. Employee Share Ownership Plans sometimes extend beyond the provision of equity in the employer company alone to more general share investments, and may become a major discretionary savings vehicle for Australian workers over coming years, supplementing the compulsory superannuation system. (See also *Employee Share Acquisition Company*).

Employer-Sponsored Fund A superannuation fund established by an employer for its employees.

EMS Abbreviation for **European Monetary System**, an agreement between member nations of the European Union to maintain an alignment between the exchange rates of their respective currencies.

Endorser A party who, for a fee, endorses a *Bill of Exchange* on its reverse as confirmation of purchase and title, thereby improving the bill's status in the market. The endorser is liable to pay on maturity the face value of the bill to its holder, should both the *acceptor* and the *drawer* fail to pay. (See also *Bank Bill*).

Enhanced Cash A portfolio management technique which aims to attain returns consistently above the prevailing cash rate by taking advantage of the higher yields available from securities with lower liquidity and credit ratings than conventional *liquid assets*.

EPS Abbreviation for *Earnings per Share*.

Equitisation The use of *futures contracts* to convert cash investments into effective exposure to equity markets.

Equity a) A synonym for a share (as distinct from fixed interest) investment; b) The interest or value which an owner has in an asset over and above the debt against it.

Equity Risk Premium The difference between the rate of return available from *risk-free assets* (such as Government bonds) and that available from assuming the risk inherent in more volatile investment such as shares. Over the very long term in Australia, the equity risk premium is around 8% over cash. Shorter term it is of the order of 3% over long bonds, which are themselves some 2% over cash.

Equity Swap See *Swap*.

Equity Trust A form of *unit trust* in which unitholders' funds are invested in shares.

ERF Abbreviation for *Eligible Rollover Fund*.

ERISA Abbreviation for **Employee Retirement Income Security Act,** landmark 1974 legislation governing the United States pension market. The 'ERISA market' thus refers to United States Pension funds.

ESAC Abbreviation for *Employee Share Acquisition Company.*

ESOP Abbreviation for *Employee Share Ownership Plan.*

ESP Abbreviation for *Eligible Service Period.*

ETC Abbreviation for *Electronic Trade Confirmation System.*

Ethical Investment An investment approach which takes into account considerations other than solely the financial return potential of particular investments. An ethical investment policy might include, for instance, a decision to avoid investing in certain sectors (eg. alcohol and tobacco), or to positively favour investments in others (eg. companies which manufacture environmentally-friendly products).

ETP Abbreviation for *Eligible Termination Payment.*

Eurodollars US dollar deposits placed with banks outside the United States. Holders may include individuals, companies, banks and central banks.

Euromarkets The international markets for the investment of currencies outside their country of origin and free from government interference.

European Option An *option* which may only be exercised for settlement on the expiration date. (See also *American Option*).

Excessive Component A component of an individual's *Eligible Termination Payment* which exceeds his or her *Reasonable Benefit Limit*. Excessive components of ETPs are taxed at the maximum marginal tax rate.

Excess Return The return achieved by a security over and above that obtained from a *risk-free asset* (such as a short-term government bond) held over the same period.

Exchange Controls Government regulations restricting the free exchange of the domestic currency to and from foreign currencies.

Exchange Rate The price of the currency in terms of another currency. (See also *Direct Quotation, Indirect Quotation*).

Exchange Risk The risk that the value of an investment may be diminished by movements in the exchange rate on a foreign currency.

Exchange Settlement Funds Funds held in the Reserve Bank, and used by banks to settle transactions with each other, eg. cheques after they have been cleared.

Exchange Traded Option An *option* over *ordinary shares* created and traded on the Stock Exchange. (See also *Over-the-Counter Option*).

Excluded Fund A superannuation fund or approved deposit fund which is exempt from operation of the *SIS Legislation,* ie. because it has fewer than five members in the case of a superannuation fund, or has only one beneficiary or meets other prescribed conditions in the case of an *Approved Deposit Fund.*

Ex-Dividend A term meaning 'without dividend': denotes a share price which is quoted on the basis that the seller, not the buyer, is entitled to the current dividend on the share. (Opposite of *Cum Dividend*).

Execute an Order To fulfil an order to buy or sell. When an execution is referred to as 'good', it generally means that both the broker and the customer are satisfied that the price obtained is fair.

Exercise The act of converting an *option* into its underlying commodity or security.

Exercise Price The price at which an option holder has the right to buy (in the case of a *call option*) or sell (in the case of a *put option*) the underlying commodity, currency or investment instrument. The term is used interchangeably with the term **Strike Price**.

Exit Fee A fee charged in relation to some pooled investments for redemptions of units (withdrawals) by unitholders. (See also *Redemption Fee*).

Expected Rate of Return The weighted arithmetic average of all possible returns on an asset or portfolio, where the weights represent the probabilities that each outcome will occur. It is the *expected value* or *mean* of a probability distribution.

Expected Value A statistical term denoting a predicted value of a future variable.

Expiration Date The date on which the right to buy or sell a security under an *option* expires.

Ex Post A statistical term denoting backward-looking, or historical, variables.

Exposure Risk The risk associated with investments in a particular industry sector, country, company, etc. Assessments of exposure risk are routinely conducted by responsible investors, as some risk element is inherent in all forms of investment other than cash.

Ex Rights A share which is trading such that buyers do not receive the right to a new issue, usually resulting in a lower price. (Opposite of *Cum Rights*).

External Audit Examination of an organisation's financial records and operations by an independent, external party. (See also *Audit, Internal Audit*).

External Manager An organisation (eg. an investment management company) engaged to manage and invest funds on behalf of a client (eg. a Government authority or trustees of superannuation funds).

Extrinsic Value The price of an *option* less its *intrinsic value*. The entire premium of an *out-of-the-money option* consists of extrinsic value. It is therefore the option's *time value*.

Face Value The value of a bond that appears on the face of the bond, unless the value is otherwise specified by the issuer. Face value is ordinarily the amount that the issuer promises to pay at maturity and is not an indication of current market value.

Factor An aspect of the investment environment which influences returns on financial assets. (See also *Common Factor*).

Fair Market Value a) The price at which a buyer and seller agree to conduct a transaction; b) The value of an *option* or *futures premium* according to a mathematical model.

FAST Abbreviation for *Flexible Accelerated Securities Transfer*.

FBT Abbreviation for *Fringe Benefits Tax*.

Federal Reserve The Fed, as it is also known, was established by the US Congress in 1913 and comprises 12 regional Federal Reserve banks, the largest being the Federal Reserve Bank of New York. These regional banks are governed by the Federal Reserve Board, and together act as the US *central bank*.

Feeder Fund See *Master Fund*

FID Abbreviation for *Financial Institutions Duty*.

Fidelity Cover A type of insurance against loss of money held in trust for or on behalf of investors. Fidelity cover must be maintained by all stock exchanges, funded by contributions from the exchange's members.

Fiduciary A person or organisation entrusted with the responsibility of managing, holding or investing assets in the best interests of the owner of the assets. Trustees of superannuation funds are fiduciaries in respect of the members of their funds.

Fifty (50) Leaders Index A *share price index* measuring price movements in 50 leading stocks listed on the Australian Stock Exchange. (See also *All Ordinaries Index*).

Fifty Leaders Index 1980-1995

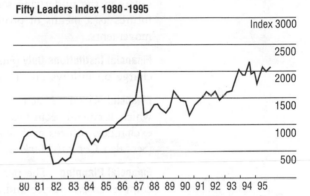

Financial Analyst An expert trained to advise on the risk and return characteristics of investments and on the management of investment portfolios.

Financial Asset Any *asset* that can be *securitised*, ie. represented by a written certificate (eg. a *share certificate* or *bond*) that establishes a claim on the issuing person or organisation.

Financial Futures   Futures contracts concerned with transactions of financial instruments, as distinct from physical commodities. Financial futures available in Australia include bank bill futures, Share Price Index (SPI) futures and Commonwealth bond futures. The essential value of financial futures is that they allow investors to hedge against adverse movements in interest rates or share prices. Financial futures can also be used by *speculators* who, while having no involvement as buyers or sellers in the underlying securities, can trade in futures as a means of profiting from expected price movements.

Financial Institutions Duty (FID)   A State Government charge on inflows into financial institutions.

Financial Market   A generic term for the markets in which financial securities are traded, eg. stock exchanges, futures exchanges, currency markets. (See also *Capital Markets, Money Market*).

Financial Planning   The process of providing comprehensive advice and assistance to a client for the purpose of meeting a client's financial needs and life goals. The process normally includes six steps: data gathering, goal setting, identification of financial issues, preparation of written options and recommendations implementation of the client's decision, and periodic review and revision of the plan.

Financial Planning Association of Australia (FPA)   The national body representing professionals who specialise in giving *financial planning* advice, with 700 members, including 320 principal members (licensed dealers or investment advisers). FPA funds an independent cost-free Complaints Code of Ethics and Rules of Professional Conduct and holds the exclusive licence in Australia to confer the international designation of Certified Financial Planner.

FINANCIAL PLANNING
ASSOCIATION OF
AUSTRALIA LIMITED
PRINCIPAL MEMBER

Firm Bid   A bid to buy a security at a definite price with the understanding that it will hold good for a certain period of time. (See also *Firm Offer*).

Firm Commitment   An arrangement under which the *underwriter* of an issue of securities undertakes to purchase all of the issue not taken up by the general public.

Firming of the Market   A period when security prices tend to rise from a depressed condition or to stabilise at current levels.

Firm Offer   An offer to sell a security at a definite price with the understanding that it will hold good for a certain period of time. (See also *Firm Bid*).

Firm Price   A stated price which the maker of a *firm bid* or *firm offer* is obliged to meet if the bid or offer is accepted within the specified time.

Fiscal Policy   The aspect of Government economic policy dealing with tax, welfare payments and government expenditure. (See also *Monetary Policy*).

Fixed Assets

Fixed Assets See *Assets*.

Fixed Income American term for *Fixed Interest*.

Fixed Interest Referring to income which remains constant and does not fluctuate, such as income derived from *bonds*, *annuities* and *preference shares*. Any *debt security* which has a fixed flow of income is known as a fixed interest security.

Flexible Accelerated Securities Transfer (FAST) The electronic share settlement system used by the Australian Stock Exchange prior to the introduction of the *CHESS* system in 1995.

Float a) In relation to currencies, the exposure of the currency to fluctuations in market forces rather than having a fixed value set by government; b) In relation to companies, the decision to put a company's shares on offer to the public (See also *Initial Public Offering, Placement*).

Floating Rate An interest rate which moves in line with market or benchmark rates instead of remaining constant for the life of a loan.

Floating Rate Notes See *FRNs*.

Floor The trading area where securities are bought and sold on an exchange. It is far less of the bull pit it used to be since the advent of *screen trading*.

Floor Price The lowest price which a seller is prepared to accept, eg. the reserve price at an auction.

Floor Return An assured minimum investment return, which leaves the investor free to participate in higher returns should interest rates or investment performance exceed the floor level. *Capital protected* investment products typically offer a floor return. (See also *Upside Capture*).

Foreign Investment Funds (FIF) Tax A tax on unrealised gains made by Australian investors in certain offshore investments. The aim of the tax, introduced in 1992, is to prevent perceived abuses of the taxation system during the 1980s, under which income could be earned overseas, taxed at favourable rates and never returned to Australia.

Foreign Securities Securities issued by foreign governments or companies incorporated outside Australia.

Forward Referring to future commitments with regard to prices (commodity, currency, or investment instrument) for which terms are established in the present.

Forward Contract A cash market transaction in which two parties agree to the purchase and sale of a commodity at some future time under such conditions as the two agree. In contrast to *futures contracts*, the terms of forward contracts are not standardised, a forward contract is not transferable and there is no margin or *collateral* requirement to assure performance of the contract.

Forward Interest Rate The prevailing interest rate for a contract in a specific future time period.

Forward Margin The difference between the current (or *spot*) price and its projected future price (forward rate).

Forward Rate Agreement (FRA) A contract for borrowing or lending at a stated interest rate over a stated time period that begins at some time in the future. FRAs are used by parties wishing to protect themselves against future interest-rate movements.

FPA Abbreviation for *Financial Planning Association of Australia.*

FRA Abbreviation for *Forward Rate Agreement.*

Franked Dividends Dividends on shares with *imputation credits* attached. A company is able to declare that a percentage (up to 100%) of a dividend is franked depending on the amount of tax the company has already paid. If a company pays the full company tax rate, the dividends are **fully franked.** (See also *Dividend Imputation, Imputation Credit*).

Friendly Society A type of mutual organisation first established in the nineteenth century. Many friendly societies have now come to operate in a similar manner to *life insurance companies.* Friendly Societies fall under the supervision of the Australian Financial Institutions Commission.

Friendly Society Bond An investment product similar to an *insurance bond,* issued by a friendly society. Originally invested only in cash and similar investments, these bonds now include investments in fixed interest securities, equities, property and a whole range of risk assets. (See also *Insurance Bond*).

Fringe Benefits Tax (FBT) A tax on non-salary benefits that is paid by employers on behalf of their employees. Such benefits may include everything from parking to company cars and subsidised home mortgage payments.

FRNs Abbreviation for **Floating Rate Notes**, being long-term (5 years or more) debt securities whose interest rates are adjusted periodically in line with a benchmark rate. FRNs appeal to investors who might otherwise be reluctant to commit funds to fixed interest investments for lengthy periods in times of fluctuating interest rates.

Front End Fee A fee charge to a borrower at the commencement of a loan, or a commission levied on an investor to buy into a unit trust. Also known as **front-end load.**

Front Office A term that refers to the main business activities of a company, as opposed to the operational or 'back office' operations. For example, the front office of an investment bank comprises the analysts, dealers and traders, while the back office comprises the accounting, reporting and support operations. A clear demarcation between front office and back office helps ensure that appropriate *Chinese Walls* exist within a financial services organisation and that its business activities are properly accountable and appropriately monitored and recorded.

FT Index Abbreviation for *Financial Times Index,* an index measuring movements in shares of 30 industrial companies listed on the London Stock Exchange.

FTSE Abbreviation for *Financial Times Stock Exchange Index,* the United Kingdom equivalent of the US *S&P500 Index* and the Australian *All Ordinaries Index*. The FTSE lists the 100 largest public companies traded on the London Stock Exchange. Usually referred to in the trade as 'Footsie'.

FTSE Index 1980 -1995

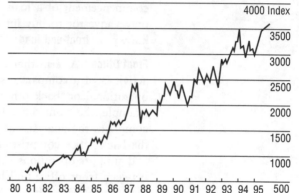

Full Vesting The inclusion in an employee's superannuation benefit of the total amount of the employer's contribution. (See also *Vesting*).

Fully Funded Referring to a superannuation fund in which the assets and liabilities are at least equal. In other words, all obligations to members can be met at any point in time. Opposite of *Unfunded Liabilities*.

Fundamental Analysis Analysis of share values based on factors such as sales, earnings and assets that are 'fundamental' to the enterprise of the company in question. These factors are considered in light of current share prices to ascertain any mispricing of the shares.

Fund Manager See *Investment Manager*.

Fund of Funds See *Master Fund*.

Fungibility The characteristic of interchangeability. For instance, *futures contracts* for the same commodity and delivery month are fungible due to their standardised specifications for quality, quantity, delivery date and delivery locations.

Futures See *Futures Contract*.

Futures Contract An obligation to make or take delivery of a specified quantity and quality of an underlying asset at a particular time in the future and at a price agreed when the contract was executed. (See also *Financial Futures*).

Futures Exchange A market in which *futures contracts* are transacted. A number of futures exchanges exist overseas for trading in physical commodity futures, eg. wheat, cotton, sugar, as well as *financial futures*. In Australia, the *Sydney Futures Exchange* has operated since 1960, dealing firstly in wool futures, then gold and other commodities including live cattle and finally moving into *financial futures* in the late 1970s after overcoming Commonwealth Treasury objections.

Futures Option An *option* (either *put* or *call)* on a futures contract.

FX Abbreviation for *Foreign Exchange* (ie. currency) dealing.

FX Option Another term for *Currency Option*.

GAAP Abbreviation for *Generally Accepted Accounting Principles*.

Gamma The way in which an option's or portfolio's *delta* changes as the value of the underlying instrument changes.

Gapping See *Jumping*.

GATT Abbreviation for *General Agreement on Tariffs and Trade*.

GDP Abbreviation for *Gross Domestic Product*.

Gearing a) A measure of indebtedness, ie. the extent of borrowings as against the equity held by a person or company in an asset; b) The ability to increase exposure by investing in *futures contracts* without making the underlying cash available. (See also *Leverage*).

General Agreement on Tariffs and Trade (GATT) Struck in 1947 to reduce international trade barriers and establish fair trading standards, GATT has evolved into a quasi international trade organisation, with 88 member countries and its own offices in Geneva. There have been eight rounds of trade negotiations since GATT was established, the most recent being the Uruguay Round completed in 1993 which reduced barriers to agricultural trade.

Generally Accepted Accounting Principles (GAAP) A set of accounting rules established and recognised by international accounting authorities.

Geometric Average A compounded average rate of return that is time weighted for a specified time period. Geometric averages are often used for measuring the performance of an investment portfolio, adjusted for the timing of new deposits and withdrawals.

Gilt Edged Low risk investments with high security.

Gilts Domestic bonds issued in the United Kingdom by the United Kingdom Government.

Global Custodian See *Custodian*.

GNP Abbreviation for *Gross National Product*.

Gold Standard A monetary system where a country's currency is valued and convertible into a fixed quantity of gold.

'Good' Funds Assets that banks are always willing to receive from other banks to represent final payment of claims. Currency and, especially, deposits at the central bank constitute good funds.

Goods and Services Tax (GST) A tax on individual goods and/or services, which is added on to the retail price of those goods or services. Goods and services taxes are often advocated as a means of increasing savings in the economy as an alternative to income taxes, which are perceived to penalise savings and to reward spending. Also known as **Consumption Tax** or, in some countries, **Value Added Tax**.

Government Bank See *Central Bank*.

Greenback A colloquial term for the United States dollar.

Greenmail A term that describes when a hostile bidder threatens a company with takeover by purchasing a large number of its shares, forcing the management of the company to repurchase the shares at an above market price.

Gross The total, before deductions have been taken away. (Opposite of *Net*).

Gross Domestic Product (GDP) A measurement in dollar terms of the aggregate goods produced and services provided within an economy over a year and excluding income earned outside the country. Considered one of the main yardsticks of the health and vitality of an economy. (See also *Gross National Product*).

Gross National Product (GNP) An economic statistic which includes *GDP* plus any income earned by residents from their overseas investments, minus income earned within the domestic economy by overseas residents.

Group of Seven (G7) The seven major capitalist powers: Canada, France, Germany, Italy, Japan, the United Kingdom and the United States. Their finance ministers meet every two years to compare and coordinate monetary policies and exchange rate information.

G7 See *Group of Seven*.

Growth Assets A general term for assets such as shares and property, which provide investment returns, (comprising both capital growth and income), which outperform inflation. Growth assets compare to *debt securities* such as fixed interest and/or cash investments.

Growth Fund An investment portfolio which aims to achieve an above average rate of after-tax income and capital growth over the medium to longer term, while adopting a medium risk profile. A growth fund typically comprises a balanced portfolio of equities, fixed interest, property and cash.

Typical Asset Allocation - Growth Fund

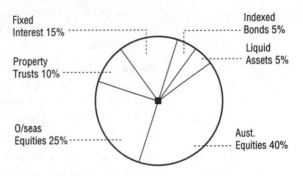

Fixed Interest 15%
Indexed Bonds 5%
Liquid Assets 5%
Property Trusts 10%
O/seas Equities 25%
Aust. Equities 40%

Growth Investor One who seeks capital gain from expected further growth in company earnings. Typically, growth investors care less about *price/earnings ratios* and other valuation measures and more about earnings growth.

GST Abbreviation for *Goods and Services Tax.*

Guarantee A requirement, eg. under a *contract,* to perform an obligation or to discharge a liability of another party in the event that the party fails to do so itself. The provider of the guarantee is known as the guarantor. Note that in the case of some *capital guaranteed* products, the guarantee is often only as good as the guarantor's surplus of assets over liabilities. (See also *Indemnity*).

Hang Seng Index The principal Hong Kong Share Price Index, equivalent to the Australian *All Ordinaries Index*.

Headline Inflation The published overall inflation rate, unadjusted for non-economic factors, as opposed to *underlying inflation*.

Head A charting term similar to a *peak*. On charts where there are several peaks in succession, the highest peak is referred to as the head, and the lower peaks on either side of the head are known as **shoulders**.

Hedge a) (Noun) An investment position taken up to counteract the risk of another position, eg. the purchase of a *put option* to offset potential losses from ownership of physical stock; b) (Verb) To take up such an investment positon.

Hedge Fund A type of investment portfolio under which the fund manager is authorised to utilise a number of higher risk investment techniques, including using *derivatives, short selling* and borrowing funds to generate a higher return. Hedge funds have become particularly common in the United States but are not prominent in the Australian investment scene at present.

Hedge Ratio A ratio, usually expressed as a decimal between 0 and 1, representing the likely movement in an *option premium* for a given move in the underlying market price of the relevant commodity, currency or investment instrument. The hedge ratio indicates how much of the underlying asset to hold against an option position in order to achieve a riskless state. (See also *Delta*).

Hedging   The practice of undertaking one investment activity in order to protect against loss in another, eg. selling short to nullify a previous purchase, or buying long to offset a previous short sale. While hedges reduce potential losses, they also tend to reduce potential profits. Typical hedges include currency *forwards* and share and bond *futures*.

Historical Volatility   The actual volatility, ie. variability in price, exhibited by an underlying instrument over an established period of time.

Holding Company   A company which owns and exercises a controlling interest in another company or companies.

Holding Period   The length of time a security is held.

Home Page   An individual or company's electronic address on the *Internet* where visual and audio information can be presented. A home page serves as a sort of electronic bulletin board where files can be posted for browsers to download. The Worldwide Web is the largest library of home pages on the Internet. Most home pages are written in *Hyper-Text Markup Language* and contain 'links' that allow users to jump to other related home pages.

Horizontal Integration   The acquisition by a company of another company which is operating in the same market. (See also *Vertical Integration*).

Household Sector   The part of the economy which is made up of individuals, families, etc. as distinct from businesses and government enterprise.

HTML   Abbreviation for *Hyper-Text Markup Language*.

Hurdle Return The minimum acceptable return an investor requires from an investment.

Hyperinflation A state of excessive *inflation*.

Hyper-Text Markup Language (HTML) The most common language used in programming Internet *home pages*.

IAB Abbreviation for *Indexed Annuity Bond*.

ICA Abbreviation for *Insurance Council of Australia*.

IFA Abbreviation for *Investment Funds Association*.

IMA Abbreviation for *Investment Management Agreement*.

IMF Abbreviation for *International Monetary Fund*.

Immunisation The design of a portfolio to achieve a target level of return in the face of changing reinvestment rates and price levels. This is done by combining short- and long-term bonds in the same portfolio to produce a predictable rate of return regardless of movements in interest rates.

Implied Volatility The level of volatility in the price of an underlying asset which is assumed for the purpose of calculating a price of an option based on that asset.

Imputation Credit Taxation credits which are passed onto shareholders who have received *franked dividends* in relation to their shareholdings. (See also *Dividend Imputation*).

IMRO Abbreviation for *Investment Management Regulatory Organisation*.

Income Portfolio A portfolio consisting of securities whose principal attractiveness lies in the steady income they provide.

Income Tax Assessment Act (ITAA) The Commonwealth legislation governing income tax, payable by Australian taxpayers.

Incorporation The legal process by which a company is established.

Indemnity A legal agreement under which one party agrees to pay for losses incurred by another. (See also *Guarantee*).

Index a) (Noun) A numerical measure of price movement in financial markets; or b) (Verb) To adjust a variable by a selected measure such as the *CPI*.

Index Arbitrage The practice of exploiting the difference between a *derivatives* market and its physical market equivalent by selling one and buying the other. Sometimes also referred to as **Program Trading**. (See also *Basis Risk*).

Indexation A means of adjusting the level of wages, prices, etc. by linking them to a selected measure, such as the level of inflation.

Indexed Annuity Bond (IAB) A form of *indexed bond* which provides a steadily-increasing stream of principal and interest payments to the holder, with a cashflow structure similar to that of a conventional mortgage. (See also *Capital-Indexed Bonds*).

Indexed Bonds Bonds which are issued with an interest rate or maturity value which is indexed to inflation rather than being fixed when the bond is issued. The most common varieties are *Capital-Indexed Bonds* and *Indexed Annuity Bonds*.

Index Fund   A portfolio of securities structured in such a way that its value will closely follow a nominated market index, eg. an equity index fund may be designed to track the *All Ordinaries Index*. There are three main methods in use: a) **Replication**, which involves buying every security in the Index in the correct proportion; b) **Stratified sampling**, which selects a sample of stocks according to simple criteria, such as size and industry grouping, to achieve an approximate tracking at lower administrative cost; and c) **Optimised sampling**, which uses a more sophisticated statistical approach involving a risk-matching process to design the best sample of stocks for any particular desired level of *tracking* accuracy. A fund structured by this method is known as an **optimised index fund**. Index funds can be designed for *equities* (domestic or overseas), *bonds*, or *property trusts*.

Indicator   A signal or statistic used to predict the value (or movement in the value) of another variable. For example, change in *Average Weekly Earnings* might be an indicator of a movement in the inflation rate.

Indirect Quotation   An exchange rate quotation in which the local currency is the base currency and the foreign currency is the terms currency, eg. GBP/USD in the United Kingdom. (See also *Direct Quotation*).

Individual Portfolio   A portfolio of investments managed on behalf of a single organisation or individual, as opposed to a pooled investment vehicle. Individual portfolios are generally only made available by professional investment managers to clients with several million dollars to invest.

Industrial Relations Commission (IRC)   The Federal Government organisation responsible for the prevention, conciliation and arbitration of industrial disputes, in particular disputes related to federal *awards*.

Industrial Shares   Shares of companies engaged in the production or sale of goods or services, as distinct from resource or mining companies. Industrials make up about two thirds of the Australian sharemarket by *market capitalisation*. (*Resource shares* make up the other third). These industrial shares are classified as the **Industrial Sector** in the *All Ordinaries Index*.

Industry Fund   A superannuation fund which is industry or union-based. Industry funds commenced general operation in 1987 following the incorporation of superannuation entitlements into many industry *awards*, although the Seafaring, Stevedoring, Storemen and Pulp and Paper industries have long-standing industry superannuation funds. Examples of industry funds are C+BUS (for Building Unions and the Construction Industry), HESTA (for the Health industry) and REST (Retail Employees' Superannuation Trust). (See also *Award Superannuation*).

Inflation   An increase in the level of prices of goods and services in the economy. It is typically measured by examining a basket of goods and services (eg. by the *Consumer Price Index*). (See also *Headline Inflation* and *Underlying Inflation*).

Inflation Hedge   A type of investment whose value can be expected to increase in a time of rising inflation. *Indexed bonds* are considered a good inflation hedge over the long term.

Information Ratio   A statistical ratio of a variable against a *standard deviation*. In relation to managed investments, information ratios are most often used to measure a manager's performance in terms of both risk and return relative to a *benchmark* or other measure (eg. the inflation rate).

Infrastructure   A general term for facilities and services required by the community and for production (eg. transport power, roads, telecommunications, water supply).

Infrastructure Bonds   A form of security supported by taxation concessions from the Australian Government, with the aim of encouraging private funding of public infrastrucutre projects in the areas of land transport, airports, seaports, gas pipelines, water supply, sewerage or waste water installations and electricity generation. Interest payments on eligible infrastructure bonds are not tax-assessable to the bondholder or deductible to the issuer and, since amendments in 1994, can also provide a tax rebate to investors on low taxation rates, such as superannutation funds. Investors can use the bond interest rebate to reduce their overall tax liability from other investments. They are administered by the *Development Allowance Authority*, which refers to them by the marketing term **Develop Australia Bonds.**

In House   Referring to an activity which is conducted within an organisation rather than contracted out to an external party. In relation to superannuation funds, the term is also used to distinguish assets which are invested directly by the employer or the trustees from those that are managed externally. Under the *SIS Legislation,* trustees of regulated superannuation funds are restricted to holding 5% or less of their investments in 'in house' assets.

Initial Public Offering (IPO)   The first sale of shares of a company to the public.

Initiation Date   The date on which an *option* contract is entered into.

Inscribed Stock   A type of stock whose ownership details are recorded in a central registry, with the owner holding a certificate which is not itself transferable. Opposite of a *bearer* security.

Insider Trading   The illegal practice of trading in securities on the basis of 'inside' or secret information which is not available to the public at large.

Insolvency   The inability of a corporation to pay debts as they fall due owing to an excess of liabilities over assets.

Institute of Actuaries of Australia   A professional association for *actuaries* which provides training for members and promotes the discussion of actuarial issues within the industry and in the wider commercial community. The Institute also aims to foster and support the ongoing development of actuarial science in Australia and throughout the Asia-Pacific region.

Institute of Chartered Accountants in Australia   A professional organisation formed in 1928, representing mainly accountants in practices. The institute is jointly responsible, with the *Australian Society of Certified Practising Accountants (ASCPA),* for the formulation and issuing of the accounting standards through the *Australia Accounting Research Foundation (AARF).*

Institutional Investor   An organisation whose primary purpose in investment markets is to invest its own assets or those held in trust by it for others. Includes superannuation funds, life companies, universities, banks, etc. Institutional investing has an ever increasing impact on securities trading. (See also *Australian Investment Managers' Association*).

Insurance   A contractual arrangement under which one party (the insurer) agrees to pay an amount of money to another (the policy holder) on the occurrence of a defined event, in return for payment of a *premium* (eg. life, disability, professional indemnity).

Insurance and Superannuation Commission (ISC)   The Commonwealth Government body with the main responsibility for regulation of the insurance and superannuation industries. Under the *SIS Legislation* the ISC assumes responsibility for certain aspects of superannuation regulation formerly conducted by the *Australian Securities Commission* (eg. disclosure requirements for *public offer funds*).

Insurance Bond   An investment product issued by life insurance companies which, if held for ten years or more, is not subject to further taxation on its final proceeds. An insurance bond policy does not necessarily include any life insurance cover for its holder. (See also *Friendly Society Bond*).

Insurance Council of Australia (ICA) An industry association established in 1975, representing general insurers in Australia. The main role of the ICA is to promote discussion of industry issues, lobby government and promote the industry to the community. (See also *Life Investment and Superannuation Association*).

Intangible Assets See *Assets*.

Interest The return earned on funds which have been loaned or invested (ie. the amount a borrower pays to a lender for the use of his/her money). (See also *Compound Interest* and *Simple Interest*).

Interest Assumption The expected rate of investment return (for actuarial purposes) on a superannuation scheme or other investment portfolio.

Interest Coverage A measure of a company's ability to meet its interest obligations, calculated by dividing interest payments into income. The higher the ratio the better.

Interest Rate Cycle A *business cycle* concerned specifically with the rise and fall of interest rates. Using historic interest rate cycles and other economic *indicators*, business analysts attempt to construct *yield curve* forecasts.

Interest Rate Futures A transferable agreement to make or take delivery of a fixed-interest security at a specific time, under terms and conditions established by a market upon which futures trading is conducted. The *Sydney Futures Exchange* offers interest rate futures contracts in 10 year and 3 year Government bonds, and in bank bills.

Interest-Rate Risk   The risk borne by fixed-interest securities, and by borrowers with floating rate loans, when interest rates fluctuate. When interest rates rise, the market value of fixed-interest securities declines and vice versa.

Interest Rate Sensitivity   The degree of movement in the price of a security, usually that of a bond, resulting from moves in interest rates. (See also *Duration*).

Interest Rate Swap   See *Swap*.

Internal Audit   An "in-house"audit of an organisation's records, procedures or systems. Unlike *external audits,* internal audits are normally conducted by the organisation's own employees or specialists it engages for the task. Their typical aims are to prevent fraud within the organisation and ensure that Board policies are being fully complied with.

Internal Rate of Return (IRR)   The rate of *discount* which needs to be applied to make the *net present value* of an investment equal to the price paid.

International Monetary Fund (IMF)   An international organisation founded in 1947 to promote maintenance of equilibrium in the balance of payments among the various nations of the world. The functions of the IMF include the levying of quotas on member nations to create a pool of funds available to be loaned to nations facing balance of payments problems.

International Organisation of Securities Commissions (IOSCO) An association of securities commissions and stock exchanges that aims to enhance regulation of financial markets, on a domestic as well as international level, through cooperation and information exchange. IOSCO was established in 1987 with its head office in Montreal, Canada. As at April 1996, IOSCO had 120 member agencies (73 voting, 10 associate and 37 affiliate) from 78 countries. The *Australian Securities Commission* and *Australian Stock Exchange* are members of IOSCO.

Internet A global electronic communication network of linked computer servers. At present, it is used mainly to exchange electronic mail and to access the Worldwide Web, the Internet library of *home pages*. Although local access to the Internet is heavily influenced by universities and telecommunications companies, there is no global governing agency. As such, there is currently no way of guaranteeing the confidentiality of information exchanged, a major impediment to wider use of the Internet in the finance industry.

In-the-Money Option A *call option* whose *exercise price* is below, or a *put option* whose exercise price is above, the current price of the asset on which the option is written.

Intrinsic Value a) The actual money value which an object possesses in itself (ie. its value in relation to unsatisfied demand). As applied to securities, intrinsic value is the basic worth of a corporation, as calculated by its past record and potential earning power; b) In relation to a *call (put) option*, the amount by which the *exercise price* is less (more) than the market price. It is the value of an option if it is exercised immediately.

Inverted Market In relation to *futures* trading, a market in which prices for distant futures are below the prices of the nearer futures. (See also *Backwardation*).

Invest Australia See *Development Allowance Authority*.

Investible Capable of being invested. When comparing investment returns against a *benchmark*, it is preferable that the benchmark be an investible one in order that realistic comparisons can be made between actual and benchmark performance.

Investment An asset acquired for the purpose of producing income and/or *capital gains* for its owner.

Investment Analyst A financial expert trained to analyse the activities and future prospects and earnings of companies and securities for the purpose of investment.

Investment Environment The general economic, political, legal and market conditions within which an investment is made.

Investment Fluctuation Reserve A pool of reserves kept within a superannuation fund, created by retaining a proportion of returns when returns are high, to be utilised to supplement payments to members when returns are low. This allows member payments to be more consistent. (See also *Smoothing*).

Investment Funds Association of Australia (IFA)　An industry association established in 1985 representing retail investment managers. The main role of the association is to educate members and the wider community, compile industry statistics, establish practice standards and make representations to Government on issues affecting the interests of the managed funds industry.

Investment Grade Bonds　Bonds which have a *credit rating* which is sufficient for them to be purchased by most institutional investors (particularly those whose investments are regulated).

InvestmentLink　A communications network that enables financial advisers to electronically access up to date, consolidated information in a central database of all their clients' investments, provided by participating investment product suppliers. The information includes details of client transactions, balances, fund rates, and the investment products.

Investment-linked　A term used to describe *insurance bonds* or other financial products whose returns are measured in terms of unit prices, based on the market values of the underlying assets. The term is particularly used as a term of distinction from *capital-guaranteed* products, the returns from which are determined by the life insurance company sponsoring them. (See also *Market-linked*).

Investment Management Agreement (IMA) A contractual agreement between an investor and an investment manager stating the terms and conditions applying to management of the stated assets. For the superannuation industry, the *SIS Legislation* requires that Investment Management Agreements be made in writing, and that they include provisions that the manager provide appropriate information as to its investment returns and management process, and sufficient information to enable the trustees to assess the manager's capabilities to manage their investments.

Investment Management Regulatory Organisation (IMRO) A regulatory organisation for the investment management industry in the United Kingdom.

Investment Manager An organisation that specialises in the investment of a portfolio of securities on behalf of individuals and/or organisations subject to the guidelines and directions of the investor. Investment managers offer both pooled investment products and individual portfolios to a range of clients including superannuation funds, institutions and individual investors.

Investment Mix See *Asset Allocation.*

Investment Philosophy The set of principles or systems used by investors to govern the way they manage portfolios. Sometimes confused with investment style, which tends more to be associated with the level of risk in the portfolio.

Investor A person whose principal purpose is to invest money prudently and productively over the longer term with the investment objectives being achievement of a reasonable return and capital appreciation to preserve purchasing power. The opposite of a *Speculator*, who will sacrifice safety of principal for the possibility of larger gains.

IOSCO Abbreviation for *International Organisation of Securities Commissions*.

IPO Abbreviation for *Initial Public Offering*.

IRC Abbreviation for *Industrial Relations Commission*.

IRR Abbreviation for *Internal Rate of Return*.

ISC Abbreviation for *Insurance and Superannuation Commission*.

Issued Capital That part of the *authorised capital* of a company which has been issued to shareholders.

ITAA Abbreviation for *Income Tax Assessment Act*.

J unk Bond

Jelly Roll A long *call* and short *put option* in one expiration month, and a short call and long put in a different expiration month. All four options must have the same underlying commodity, stock, or index, and typically also have the same *exercise price*. The effect is to create a long synthetic position in one month offset by a short synthetic position in a different month.

Joint Venture A project undertaken by two or more parties, (eg. between a private company and a government instrumentality) to achieve a mutual objective.

Jump Non-continuous trading or prices in the underlying commodity, currency or investment instrument. Generally, this is represented by a one-off movement of extreme order in the market price. For example, the effect on *option* prices occasioned by the share market crash of October 1987. (Also known as *Gapping*).

Junk Bond A high risk, high yield *debt security* rated below triple B.

Knock In

Knock In   A *call* or *put option* that does not take effect until the *underlying security* reaches a predetermined price. There are two varieties of knock ins: 'down and ins' take effect when the underlying security falls to a certain price, and 'up and ins' take effect when the underlying security rises to a certain price. (See also *Knock Out*).

Knock Out   A *call* or *put option* that expires if the underlying security reaches a predetermined price. There are two varieties of knock outs: 'down and outs' expire if the underlying security falls to a certain price, and 'up and outs' expire if the underlying security rises to a certain price. (See also *Knock In*).

Lagging Indicators Economic variables which tend to follow movements in the economy as a whole (eg. trade figures) and whose publication confirms things that have already happened rather than pointing to emerging trends. (Opposite of *Leading Indicators*).

Last Sale The last price at which a transaction in a security took place on a certain day or a particular time during a trading session. These prices are often important for the purposes of valuing a portfolio.

Last Trading Day The final day under an Exchange's rules during which trading may take place in a particular *futures contract's* delivery month. A futures contract outstanding at the end of the last trading day must be settled by delivery of physicals or by cash settlement.

LBO Abbreviation for *Leveraged Buy-out*.

Leading Indicators Economic variables which are seen as anticipatory of future trends or expectations (eg. share prices, currency movements), as opposed to indicators which are based on retrospective or historical statistics. (Opposite of *Lagging Indicators*).

Lease An agreement between two parties allowing one party to use an asset (eg. property) owned by the other party, for a specified time period, in return for a series of payments.

Leaseback A property transaction in which the seller remains in possession of the property as a tenant after completing the sale and delivering the deed.

LEPO Abbreviation for *Low Exercise Price Option*.

Letter of Comfort   A form of reassurance that a company will be able to meet its liabilities or perform its obligations under a contract. Letters of comfort are often issued by parent companies in relation to their overseas subsidiaries. They do not necessarily amount to a formal *guarantee*.

Letter of Credit   An undertaking by a bank to repay a loan obligation in the event of a default by a subsidiary or a client company.

Leverage   a) A synonym for *gearing* (eg. using derivative investments to over-invest a portfolio); or b) The use of an asset as security for a borrowing.

Leveraged Buy-out (LBO)   The use of borrowed funds to purchase a company where the equity value or potential cash flow of the target company is expected to be sufficient to result in a profit for shareholders and/or meet debt repayments.

Liabilities   a) Debts (plus, in the case of companies, dividends due to shareholders). Opposite of *Assets*; b) A stream of obligations (eg. pension payments).

Liability Consultant   A professional person engaged by holders of liabilities, such as banks or industry superannuation funds, to advise on appropriate payment strategies and organisational structures to meet a stream of obligations. (See also *Asset Consultant*).

LIBOR   Abbreviation for *London Interbank Offered Rate*, the interest rate at which major international banks in London will lend cash to each other, and thus an indicator rate for international lending.

Lien   A charge over an asset, or the right to hold another party's assets as security for that party's performance of an obligation.

Life Insurance Act The 1945 Commonwealth legislation which is the main source of regulation of Australia's life insurance industry.

Life Insurance Company A financial institution with the main business of providing insurance against death and disability through households investing funds with the company. Life insurance companies also operate superannuation funds.

Life Investment and Superannuation Association (LISA) An industry association representing Australian and overseas-based mutual societies and proprietary direct-writing and reinsurance companies. Its objectives are to represent the interest of member companies, their policyholders and beneficiaries, and to promote public understanding of and appreciation of the benefits provided by life insurance, investment and superannuation. Membership is open to all companies registered under the Commonwealth Life Insurance Act 1995. As at June 1995, LISA had 37 members, responsible for 9.5 million life insurance and superannuation policies which were in force for a sum insured of $617 billion.

LIFE, INVESTMENT AND SUPERANNUATION
ASSOCIATION OF AUSTRALIA INCORPORATED

Life Office Another name for a *Life Insurance Company*.

Limited Liability A form of company structure under which shareholders' liabilities are limited to the value of their shares in the company, even when the debts of the company actually exceed that value.

Limit Order An order to buy or sell a stated amount of a security at a specified price, or better if obtainable, after the order is represented on the floor of the stock exchange. (See also *Market Order*).

Liquid Assets Assets held as cash, or in the form of securities which can be converted into cash swiftly and with minimal capital loss (eg. short-term bank bills). (See also *Liquidity*).

Liquidation The winding up of the affairs of a company, including sale of its assets, settlement of its liabilities (if possible) and payment of any remaining cash to shareholders. (See also *Receivership*).

Liquidator A person appointed, usually by a court, to conduct the winding-up of a company and the *liquidation* of its assets. (See also *Administrator* and *Receiver*).

Liquidity a) The ability of an investment to be easily converted into cash with little or no loss of capital and minimum delay. An example of a highly liquid asset is a short-term *bank bill* or *promissory note*, while property is a relatively illiquid investment. For many securities, the degree of liquidity depends on the depth of the *secondary market* for that security; b) The maintenance of cash and reserves by a financial institution to fund withdrawals by depositors, unitholders or clients.

Liquidity Cycle An economic observation of the way asset prices rise or fall in relation to cyclical movements in interest rates over a *business cycle*.

Liquidity Preference Theory The proposition that investors characteristically prefer *liquidity* in investments and consequently will generally only be induced to hold longer-term securities if higher returns are offered. The theory is used to explain the term structure of interest rates. (See also *Risk Premium*).

Liquidity Premium An additional price paid for an asset on the basis of its greater liquidity or tradeability or, alternatively, an additional return required by an investor to compensate for lack of liquidity.

Liquidity Risk The risk that an investment may not be easily converted into cash with little or no loss of capital and minimum delay.

Liquid Market A market where selling and buying can be accomplished with ease, due to the presence of a large number of interested buyers and sellers willing and able to trade substantial quantities at small price differences.

LISA Abbreviation for *Life Investment and Superannuation Association*.

Listed Company A company whose shares are traded on the stock exchange and are able to be bought and sold by members of the general public.

Listed Property Trust (LPT) See *Property Trust*.

Listed Security A security which is traded on an exchange for the organised buying and selling of securities (eg. shares on the stock exchange, or futures on the futures exchange). Listed securities are usually more liquid than unlisted ones owing to the existence of such an exchange. (See also *Secondary Market*).

Listing Rules Rules set out by the *Australian Stock Exchange* with which companies must comply to remain eligible to be listed companies.

Local A member of *a futures* exchange with the authority to deal on the trading floor on his/her own account or for Floor Members but not on behalf of clients.

Lognormal Distribution The standard statistical model for the expected distribution of asset price movements. More technically, it assumes that the natural logarithms of relative price movements are normally distributed.

Lombard A rate of interest set by the German *Bundesbank* that is used specifically for loans to commercial banks. The Lombard rate is generally half a percentage point higher than the *discount rate*.

London Interbank Offered Rate See *LIBOR*.

Long In relation to foreign exchange and share market trading, referring to an ownership position in which the trader has bought more of a particular security than he or she has sold.

Long Position An excess of purchases over sales of the relevant commodity, currency or investment instrument. (Opposite of *Short Position*).

Look Back Option An *option* whose exercise or strike price depends on the prices reached prior to its expiry; eg. the minimum value reached during the option period.

Lot Usually a specific quantity of a standard grade of a commodity, or a unit of trading equivalent to one futures contract.

Low Exercise Price Option (LEPO) A derivative contract developed by the Australian Stock Exchange in 1994 that has a lower exercise price and, as a result, provides greater leverage than a standard *call option*. Its premium moves almost dollar for dollar with the price of the underlying share, not by differing amounts dependent on the time to expiry. This greater leverage entails greater risk. LEPOs are monitored daily like futures, and both buyers and sellers are subject to possible *margin calls*. LEPOs also have a *European option* expiry, unlike standard call options, which further increases their risk profile. At the time of going to print (April 1996), contracts were available for ten underlying shares.

LPT Abbreviation for *Listed Property Trust*.

Lump Sum In relation to superannuation, a benefit payable in cash rather than as a *pension* or *annuity*.

Lump Sum Reasonable Benefit Limit See *Reasonable Benefit Limit*.

Lump Sum Tax The taxation payable on the lump-sum component of a superannuation payout.

Maastricht Treaty   A treaty signed in 1992 by members of the European Community (EC), under which the European Union (EU) was formed. The treaty calls for the establishment of European Monetary Union (EMU) by 1999 and for common policies on foreign affairs, security, justice, transport and the environment. At the time of going to print (April 1996), none of the 12 EU countries had yet met the five economic 'convergence' targets, including common GDP-deficit ratios, that have been set for 1997 as a foundation for EMU. The EU comprises Belgium, Denmark, France, Germany, Greece, Ireland, Italy, Luxembourg, the Netherlands, Portugal, Spain and the United Kingdom.

Macro Economics   Economic analysis concerning broad trends and influences on the economy, such as the interaction of *fiscal* and *monetary* policies, GDP, *balance of payments*, etc; as opposed to *micro economics*, which focuses on individual units such as companies and markets to assess their influence on the economy.

Making a Market   A dealer is said to be making a market in a given security when he or she is prepared to buy or sell at the bid and offer prices that he or she quotes. The market is maintained when he or she continues to quote bids and offerings over a period of time. Such a dealer is referred to as a **market maker**.

Management Agreement   An agreement between an investor and an investment manager stating the terms and conditions applying to management of the stated assets. (See also *Mandate*).

Management Buy-in (MBI) The purchase of a business by an external management team. MBIs are riskier than *management buy-outs*, because the new management team is not as familiar with the business, but are still attractive to institutional or professional *development capital* investors because the new management team has a personal financial interest in the company's profitability.

Management Buy-out (MBO) The purchase of a business by its management team, normally with the financial assistance of an institutional investor. MBOs are often targeted as suitable investments by *development capital* practitioners. (See also *Leveraged Buy-out*).

Management Expense Ratio (MER) A ratio expressing the management, trustee and certain other expenses of a collective investment fund as a proportion of the *net asset value* of the fund.

Mandate The agreed objectives given by an investor to his or her investment manager, often including a *benchmark portfolio*, guidelines as to maximum and minimum sector exposures, and prohibited investments. A mandate is usually set out as part of the *Management Agreement* between a fund manager and its client.

Margin a) A deposit lodged with an exchange or clearing house as collateral to cover adverse movements in market prices of an *open position*; or b) In foreign currency markets, the difference between the buying and selling rates of a foreign exchange quotation. (See also *Spread*).

Marginal Tax Rate The rate of tax payable on the top proportion of income derived by a person. In Australia at the time of going to print (April 1996), the highest marginal rate of income tax was 47% for income over $50,000, plus the Medicare Levy.

Margin Call A requirement by a clearing house that a clearing member (or by a brokerage firm that a client) brings margin deposits up to a required minimum level to cover an adverse movement in price in the futures market.

Marked to Market Value The valuation or quotation of an instrument or contract in relation to current market rates.

Marketable Parcel The minimum number of shares of a stock that can be traded.

Marketable Securities Securities for which there is always a ready market available, such as active, listed shares. (See also *Liquid Asset*).

Market Capitalisation The sum of the total amount of various securities issued by a corporation, multiplied by the current market price of those securities. It is a measure of a company's *capitalisation* in strictly market price terms, as opposed to the price those securities could fetch *off market*.

Market Cycle A *business cycle* concerned specifically with rises and falls in market activity, as measured by an *index*. Market cycles generally correspond to the *economic clock*, with periods of heavy purchasing indicating growth, and periods of heavy selling indicating recession.

Market Excess Return   The percentage excess that a particular security is forecast to earn over a *risk-free* (ie. *Treasury Note*) *rate of return*.

Market-linked   A term used to describe pooled investment schemes which are valued by reference to current movements in markets, rather than on the basis used by *capital guaranteed* funds.

Market Maker   See *Making a Market*.

Market-on-close   A stock or *options* market order to be filled at the current market price as close as possible to the close of that day's trading.

Market Order   An immediate order to buy or sell a security at the most advantageous price available after the order reaches the trading floor.

Market Price   With reference to a security, the last reported price at which the security sold. Alternatively, the highest price which a buyer, willing but not compelled to buy, would pay, and the lowest a seller, willing but not compelled to sell, would accept.

Market Risk   Risk that relates to the market as a whole and therefore cannot be diversified away simply by holding a greater variety of securities. (See also *Systematic Risk*).

Market Timing   The purchase or sale of securities on the basis of shorter-term price patterns and temporary market opportunities as well as judgements of underlying value. An extremely difficult thing to get right consistently.

Market Value   The current value of an item or security, as opposed to its *book value*. (See also *Mark to Market*).

Market Value Added   The increase in the *market value* of an item or security over a certain time period.

Mark to Market   To make an accounting adjustment to reflect unrealised gains and losses on *book values* of a particular investment at the end of a period.

Master Custodian   See *Custodian.*

Master Fund   An investment vehicle that enables individual investors or small superannuation funds to channel money into one or more underlying investments – most commonly wholesale or retail pooled funds operated by professional investment managers. Master funds can generally be categorised into three distinct types: a) **discretionary funds,** where the individual investor selects the underlying investment product(s) from a list drawn up by the master fund manager; b) **fund of funds,** where the investor selects a general risk profile (eg. growth, capital stable) but the master fund manager selects the underlying investments from among a range of products managed by external managers; and c) **feeder funds,** which operate similarly to fund of funds arrangements, but with the master fund manager also being responsible for managing the underlying investments. Master funds which are structured as prescribed interests are commonly referred to as **Master Trusts.** However, the term master fund encompasses the broader scope of the industry including products offered by life insurance companies.

Master Trust   See *Master Fund.*

Matching   The arrangement of assets, and the return from those assets, to meet future liabilities and obligations.

Maturity The date on which a loan, bond, mortgage or other debt or security is due to be repaid.

Maturity Date The date upon which the issuer of a bond repays principal to the bond's holder.

Maturity Structure In relation to a fixed interest portfolio, the positioning along the *yield curve*. It is measured in years to maturity of the relevant bonds held.

Maximum Deductible Contribution The maximum amount a person is permitted to pay into a superannuation scheme from his or her personal income. This contribution is indexed annually to *average weekly ordinary time earnings (AWOTE)*.

MBI Abbreviation for *Management Buy-in*.

MBO Abbreviation for *Management Buy-out*.

Mean Another term for 'average' (ie. a statistical indicator of a central tendency, giving a value around which the observations in a given sample tend to cluster). It does not, however, lead a life of its own. The statement that the average number of children in an Australian family is 2.3 does not imply that there is even a single family with 2.3 children. An aspect of central tendency is that the mean is always between the extreme values. (See also *Median*).

Mean Reversion The principle that over a period of time, the market price of a security (eg. the credit spread relative to an underlying *bond*) will revert back to its mean level. At any point in time the bond can be referred to as cheap, expensive or fair value relative to that mean level.

Means Test   An evaluation undertaken by the Government to assess if a person is eligible for social security payments, such as the age pension. The test assesses income and assets with the lower being the basis for determining the social security payment.

Median   The value (rate of return, market sensitivity, etc.) that exceeds one-half of the values in the sample and is exceeded by the other half. The median is always the middle value, as distinct from the *mean*, which represents the average value. For example, if five items cost $20, $80, $100, $300 and $500 respectively, the median value would be $100, whereas the mean or average would be $200.

Member Choice   A facility made available to the members of a superannuation fund allowing them to decide the proportion of funds to be allocated between high and low risk investment strategies, sectors and/or managers. Typically, a fund with a member choice facility will allow members the opportunity to switch between investment options at certain intervals.

Memorandum of Association   A document stating the basis upon which a company is created and established. The document includes the company's name, address, initial objectives, capital, basis and extent of external dealings and initial objectives. (See also *Articles of Association*).

MER   Abbreviation for *Management Expense Ratio*.

Merchant Bank   A financial institution that specialises in the structuring and arranging of various financial transactions for companies and projects.

Merger A form of corporate restructuring in which two companies combine into one. Unlike *takeovers*, mergers are usually negotiated by the management of the two companies concerned.

Mezzanine Finance A form of unsecured debt finance provided by *merchant banks* and *development capital* fund managers to companies which are in a growth phase, but may not have access to equity capital or are unwilling to dilute their existing shareholdings. Alternatively, traditional bank finance may not be available. (See also *Subordinated Debt*).

Micro Economics Economic analysis dealing with individual companies or markets and their impact on the economy, as opposed to *macro economics* which focuses on broader influences and trends.

Mispriced Security A security which is trading at a price which is substantially different (higher or lower) from its *intrinsic value*.

Modern Portfolio Theory (MPT) The theoretical constructs that enable investment managers to classify, estimate and control the sources of risk and return. In popular usage, the term encompasses all notions of modern investment, as well as portfolio theory. The end objective is to select optimal combinations of assets to produce the highest returns for a given level of risk, or the least risk for a given level of return.

Modified Duration The level of interest rate sensitivity resulting from small changes in the *yield to maturity* of a bond. Modified duration is measured as the interest rate sensitivity of the bond as a percentage of the bond's price; in other words it is the present value of the *duration*.

Momentum

Momentum   The tendency of an asset price to keep moving in the same direction, either upwards or downwards.

Monetary Policy   Reserve Bank actions to influence the availability and cost of money. In tandem with *fiscal policy*, monetary policy is one of the chief arms of Government economic policy. Tight monetary policy usually means higher interest rates as the scarcity of money prevails, whereas loose monetary policy is the reverse.

Money Market   The market for trade in short-term securities such as *Bills of Exchange*, *Promissory Notes* and Government and Semi-Government *bonds*. Participants in the money market include banks and other financial institutions, life offices, sharebrokers, superannuation funds and Government authorities. (See also *Capital Market*).

Money Market Account   A type of bank account which earns an interest rate comparable to that obtained in the *money market*. Banks normally require minimum account balances to be maintained and impose minimum withdrawal conditions on this type of account.

Money Market Fund   A *unit trust* or *mutual fund* which invests solely in *money market* (short-term) securities.

Money Supply   A measure of the amount of cash held by members of the public and in bank deposits. (See also *Broad Money*).

Money Weighted Rate of Return A return on an investment portfolio calculated by reference to the amount and the timing of cash flows during a given time period. This rate is an effective measure of the fund's rate of growth, giving full weight to the impact of cash flows on fund assets. It is the *internal rate of return (IRR)* of the cash flows. (See also *Time Weighted Rate of Return*).

Monopoly The control of an area of activity by a single individual or company.

Moody's A United States corporate credit ratings agency, which also operates in Australia and internationally. (See also *Australian Ratings, Standard & Poors*).

Morgan Stanley Capital International Index See *MSCI Index*.

Mortgage A form of security for a loan, in which a specific item of property is pledged by the borrower **(mortgagor)** to the lender **(mortgagee)**.

Mortgage-backed Certificates Securities backed by mortgages which have been pooled together and securitised to create marketable securities. Mortgage securities are a relatively recent innovation designed to facilitate a *secondary market* and to provide liquidity to otherwise relatively-illiquid investments in mortgages by financial institutions. (See also *AUSSIE MAC, Securitisation*).

MPT Abbreviation for *Modern Portfolio Theory*.

MSCI Index Abbreviation for **Morgan Stanley Capital International Index**, a series of country indexes of equity prices. The MSCI World Index is one standard for comparisons of international equity performance, although there are others, including the Frank Russell and Financial Times indices.

Morgan Stanley Capital Index 1980-1995

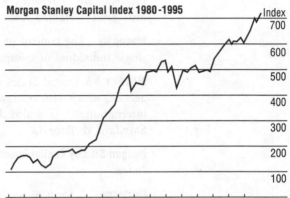

Municipal Bond The term used in the United States for a *bond* issued by a local government authority, usually with concessional taxation treatment, to pay for essential community infrastructure projects and services. The nearest equivalent to the municipal bond market in Australia is *infrastructure bonds,* which also offer investors tax concessions for investments in projects intended to benefit the broader community.

Multinational A company whose business operations and investments extend across a number of countries. Occasionally called a **Transnational Corporation**.

Mutual Fund An American term for certain forms of *collective investments*. Mutual funds are similar to Australian *unit trusts* in that individual investors are entitled to an interest in a portfolio of securities, but different in the sense that they are offered through a corporate legal structure rather than through a *trust* arrangement.

Naked Option   An option held on its own; ie. not used to *hedge* a holding in the underlying asset or another option.

National Accounts   Figures published annually in the Commonwealth Budget summarising income and expenditure for the economy as a whole and for various industry sectors. National account figures form part of the basis for calculating *Gross Domestic Product*.

National Companies and Securities Commission (NCSC) The former national regulatory authority for Australian companies and the securities and futures industries. Replaced by the *Australian Securities Commission* following commencement of the *Corporations Law* in 1991.

National Mortgage Market Corporation   A private organisation which issues *mortgage-backed certificates*; established in 1984 and based in Melbourne. (See also *AUSSIE MAC, Securitisation*).

National Savings   The total level of savings, defined as the income remaining after consumption, of a country's households.

NBFI Abbreviation for *Non-Bank Financial Institution*.

NBR Abbreviation for *Net Borrowing Requirement*.

NCSC Abbreviation for *National Companies and Securities Commission*.

Negative Gearing The purchase of an investment using borrowed funds, where the interest on the borrowing exceeds the income derived from the investment. For tax purposes, this negative net income can be offset against income gained from other sources. Negative gearing is most often associated with purchases of investment real estate, but can also apply in the case of shares or managed investments.

Negligence Failure to exercise a reasonable degree of care in relation to others, exposing them to risk of harm or injury. It has set criteria in law.

Negotiable Instrument A piece of paper representing ownership of a financial asset or debt, and capable of being traded in the *money market* (eg. *Bill of Exchange, Promissory Note*).

Net The figure remaining after all necessary deductions have been taken away. Opposite of *Gross.*

Net Asset Backing Total shareholders' funds in a company (ie. total assets less total liabilities) divided by the number of shares on issue. (See also *Asset Backing*).

Net Asset Value Total assets of a company less total liabilities. A more refined measure is **Net Tangible Assets,** which do not include intangible items like goodwill.

Net Borrowing Requirement (NBR) The total amount to be borrowed by the Government through the issuance of *Bills of Exchange* and *Bonds* to meet Government expenditure for a specific period.

Net Present Value (NPV) The current value of a stream of income discounted by a factor (usually inflation) over the period of an investment.

Net Profit The profit earned by a company less expenses such as tax and interest on borrowings. (See also *Earnings Before Interest and Tax*).

Net Realisable Value The current market price of an asset after deducting the costs of selling it.

Net Tangible Assets (NTA) See *Net Asset Value*.

Netting The practice of subtracting the amount owed by one party from the amount owed to that party and agreeing to transfer only the resulting difference.

Netting by Novation The substitution of new contractual obligations, equal to the net obligations, for the existing ones.

New Issue Any type of security issued to raise additional money. Offerings are made to existing shareholders, through *rights issues* or entitlements, and/or to non-shareholders. Proceeds may be used for retiring debt, for acquisitions or for working capital.

Nikkei Dow Index The popularly quoted Japanese Share Price Index, covering the top 225 shares listed on the Tokyo Stock Exchange. The newer, wider market measure is the *Topix*.

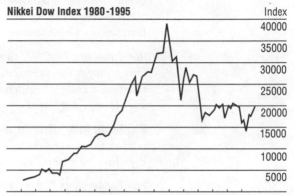

Nikkei Dow Index 1980-1995

Index
40000
35000
30000
25000
20000
15000
10000
5000

Dec 80 81 82 83 84 85 86 87 88 89 90 91 92 93 94 95

Nominal Return The rate of return in simple monetary terms, ie. unadjusted for any change in inflation. The nominal return is contrasted with the *real return*, which is adjusted for changes in inflation. A nominal interest rate of 10% is a real rate of only 6% if inflation at the time of measurement is 4%.

Nominee An individual or company in whose name a security is registered to be owned, although the real (or *beneficial*) ownership is actually held by another party. Nominee companies are often used by share investors who for some reason wish their identities to remain undisclosed or who simply require another party to manage (or hold as *custodian*) their investments.

Non-Bank Financial Institution (NBFI)

Non-Bank Financial Institution (NBFI) A generic term describing any financial institution not covered by Reserve Bank supervision, but more commonly referring to institutions such as *Building Societies, Credit Unions* and *Friendly Societies,* all of which are now regulated by the *Australian Financial Institutions Commission.*

Non-Complying Fund A superannuation fund which fails to meet the prerequisites for concessional taxation treatment under the *SIS Legislation.* (See also *Complying Fund*).

Non Factor Risk Risk in an investment which is not related to movements in *common factors* and can therefore be diversified away.

Non-Renouncable Rights Rights associated with a share that cannot be traded on the market.

Normal Distribution A statistical measure used to calculate the probability of future returns on an investment. The distribution has a characteristic 'bell' shape illustrating that the probability of returns above the mean is identical to the probability of returns below the mean (See also *Standard Deviation*).

Normal Distribution

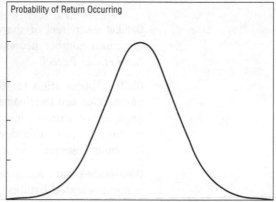

Probability of Return Occurring

Return

Novation The incorporation into existing contracts of subsequent agreements or deals between the same parties, so that at all times only one contract remains outstanding between those parties.

NPV Abbreviation for *Net Present Value*.

NTA Abbreviation for *Net Tangible Assets*.

Number One Fund See *Statutory Fund*.

Number Two Fund See *Statutory Fund*.

NZSE30 A New Zealand Share Price Index covering the top thirty shares listed on the New Zealand Stock Exchange.

Occupational Superannuation Standards Act (OSSA)
Commonwealth Government legislation passed in 1987, governing superannuation funds and establishing the former regulatory framework administered by the *Insurance and Superannuation Commission*. Much of OSSA was repealed in 1993 to make way for the new regulatory regime under the *SIS Legislation*, which took effect on 1 July 1994.

Odd Lot A parcel of shares that is below the minimum number necessary to be traded. See also *Marketable Parcel*.

OECD Abbreviation for **Organisation for Economic Co-operation and Development,** an international grouping of nations, including Australia, established to promote economic development and conduct economic research.

Off-balance-sheet Referring to financial commitments or liabilities that do not generally appear in a company's *balance sheet* (eg. operating leases or derivative contracts).

Offer The price at which a person is willing to sell. (Also known as **Ask**).

Off Market Relating to a transaction which occurs outside a formal market – eg. transactions in unlisted securities or transactions involving listed shares which were not executed on a stock exchange. Off market transactions are conducted through negotiation rather than an 'auction' system.

OPALS Abbreviation for *Optimised Portfolios As Listed Securities*.

Open-end Fund A fund in which participants buy and sell at a unit price based on the appraised value of total assets. Participants can leave and enter at any time and assets may be continually added to the fund. (Opposite of *Closed-end Fund*).

Opening Price The price at which a security commences trading at the opening of a trading day.

Open Interest The number of open contracts on a particular *option* – indicating whether the option is liquid (ie. tradeable).

Open Order An order to buy or sell at a stipulated price, which remains effective until it is executed, cancelled or changed to a different price.

Open Outcry In relation to futures markets, the method of making all bids and offers verbally in the trading pit.

Open Position In foreign exchange the situation of someone who is exposed to exchange rate movements (ie. their assets and liabilities in a particular currency do not match). The term similarly applies to *exchange-traded futures* and *options* (ie. where a buying or selling contract is not offset by its opposite position).

Operating Standards The regulatory standards under the *SIS Legislation* which must be fulfilled by Superannuation Funds, Pooled Superannuation Trusts and Approved Deposit Funds to be granted *complying fund* status by the *ISC* and to qualify for concessional taxation treatment.

Operations Risk The risk that is entailed within the operational structure of a company (eg. the separation of duties between *front office* and *back office*). It is related to the proper demarcation of responsibilities and controls on an operational level.

Optimal Portfolio   The portfolio which best meets the investor's needs and risk/return expectations among the range of all feasible portfolios.

Optimisation   A mathematical process which creates a compromise between conflicting objectives (eg. between maximising return and minimising risk). An optimisation program will identify the asset mix which is likely to give the highest return for a given risk level, or alternatively, the lowest risk portfolio to achieve a desired return. (See also *Portfolio Optimisation*).

Optimised Index Fund   See *Index Fund*.

Optimised Portfolios As Listed Securities (OPALS)   A derivatives instrument based on international equities represented by the MSCI Indices that allows investors to buy exposure to an entire overseas market in a single trade.

Optimised Sampling   See *Index Fund*.

Option   An agreement which conveys the right to the holder to buy (receive) or sell (deliver) a specific security at a stipulated price and within a stated period of time. If the option is not exercised during that time, the money paid for it (but no more than that amount) is forfeited. (See also *Call Option* and *Put Option*).

Option Buyer/Taker   The party who obtains the right conveyed by an *option*. Only the option buyer has a right to exercise the put or the call option. Opposite of *Option Writer*.

Option Premium   The dollar amount paid to the seller (writer) for an option. This amount is determined generally by supply and demand, duration of the contract and volatility of the underlying share price.

Option Strategy   The implementation of a market strategy through the use of option derivatives.

Option Trade   The purchase or sale of an option.

Option Writer   A person – usually an investor with a large portfolio – who sells *put* and/or *call option* contracts to other investors. The primary objective of the option writer is to obtain capital gain or income or to purchase stock in the future at lower than current market prices. In recent years, large financial institutions have been showing more interest in writing options against their portfolios as a way of earning more and establishing the prices at which they will buy or sell stocks.

Ordinary Shares   Securities which represent an ownership interest in a company. If the company has also issued *preference shares*, both have ownership rights. The preference shareholder normally is limited to a fixed dividend, but has prior claim on dividends and, in the event of liquidation, assets. Ordinary shareholders assume the greater risk, but generally exercise the greater control and may gain the greater reward in the form of dividends and capital appreciation. If the company is wound up, the ordinary shareholders generally rank behind secured creditors, including debenture holders, in the liquidation process.

Organistion for Economic Co-operation and Development   See *OECD*.

OSSA   Abbreviation for *Occupational Superannuation Standards Act*.

OTC Option   Abbreviation for *Over-the-Counter Option*.

Out-of-the-Money Option A call option with an *exercise price* above, or to a put option with an exercise price below, the current price of the asset on which the option is written. (Opposite of *In-the-Money Option*).

Outperformance Achievement of a higher investment return than a benchmark or other measure against which that return is being compared. For example, an equity fund would be said to have outperformed the All Ordinaries Index if the fund achieved a 5% return against a 3% return by the Index over the same period. (Opposite of *Underperformance*).

Outperformance Option An *option* where value is derived from the outperformance of one security over another predetermined security, for a specified amount invested. The owner of the option has the right to receive the additional return generated by one security compared to another, calculated on the amount invested.

Overbought Referring to a market condition under which heavy liquidation of *long positions* appears imminent. (Opposite of *Oversold*).

Overlay Manager An investment manager engaged to manage a specific aspect of an investor's portfolio (eg. currency), on an "overlay" basis through the use of derivative instruments, usually where some or all of the underlying assets are managed by other managers. (See also *Currency Overlay, Protection Overlay, and Tactical Asset Allocation Overlay*).

Oversold Referring to a market condition under which heavy liquidation of *short positions* appears overdue. (Opposite of *Overbought*).

Over-subscribed   Referring to a situation in which the value of applications received (eg. for a new share issue) exceeds the amount to be allocated.

Over-the-Counter Option (OTC Option)   Any option which is not traded on a listed exchange. It is 'tailor made' for a client by a financial institution and can only be re-sold by negotiation.

Overweight   Having a greater exposure to a particular sector or stock in an investment portfolio, compared with a neutral or benchmark position. (Opposite of *Underweight*).

Package Trade   A sharemarket transaction involving the purchase and/or sale of an entire portfolio rather than individual securities alone. Often used to manage *index funds*, and occasionally to *arbitrage* between physical and derivative securities.

PADF   Abbreviation for *Personal Approved Deposit Fund*.

Paid-up Capital   The proportion of a company's share capital which has in fact been paid for by shareholders (ie. excluding capital that has been called, but not yet paid).

Paper Profit   A profit still existing in a security which has not yet been sold, and is therefore unrealised.

Par   Referring to a foreign exchange transaction in which the forward price is the same as the spot price.

Part A Statement   A written statement, disclosing matters prescribed by the *Corporations Law,* provided by a *takeover* bidder to the *target company* shareholders for the purpose of assisting the shareholders to decide whether to accept the takeover offer.

Part B Statement   A written statement, disclosing matters prescribed by the *Corporations Law,* provided by the directors of the *target company* shareholders for the purpose of assisting them to decide whether to accept the takeover offer.

Partial Vesting   The inclusion in an employee's superannuation benefit of part of the employer's contribution, not the total amount. (See also *Vesting*).

Par Value   The face value of a security. In relation to shares, the par value is set by the company at the time of issue and does not necessarily reflect the share's market value.

Passive Management   A style of investment management that seeks to attain performance equal to the market or index returns. In pure *index funds*, no judgements are made about future market movements, although more sophisticated managers usually offer *tilted portfolios*. (Opposite of *Active Management*).

PAYE   Abbreviation for *Pay-As-You-Earn,* a taxation procedure for wage and salary earners under which income tax is deducted in instalments from periodic (ie. weekly) pay.

Pay-Off Diagram   A graphical representation of the profit and loss structure of an *option* or a combination of different option exposures. (See also *Exercise Price*).

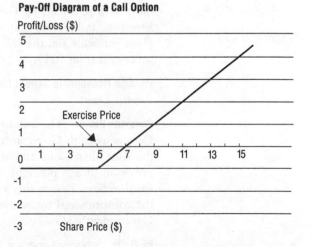

Pay-Off Diagram of a Call Option

Payout Ratio A ratio expressing the proportion of a company's profits which is paid out to shareholders in the form of *dividends*. The ratio is calculated by dividing the dividends by the amount of the company's profit. (See also *Earnings Per Share*).

Payroll Tax A State Government tax on businesses, levied on the basis of the number of employees of the business.

PDF Abbreviation for *Pooled Development Fund*.

Peak A charting term, also known as a **top** (eg. in charting prices, a peak is the point where the price climaxes before the pressure to sell pushes it back down). See also *Trough*.

Pension A regular periodic payment to a person, either by the Government (ie. social security) or as a superannuation benefit.

Pension Fund a) A superannuation fund in which benefits are payable as an income stream during retirement rather than (or as well as) by way of a lump sum payment; b) The term used in the United Kingdom and United States for retirement savings plans generally (ie. the US equivalent of superannuation funds).

Pension Reasonable Benefit Limit See *Reasonable Benefit Limit*.

Pensions Power The authority of the Commonwealth Government, under Section 51 of the Australian Constitution, to regulate the provision of age pensions. Along with the *Corporations Power,* the pensions power is one of the constitutional foundations of the federal Government's *SIS Legislation*.

PE Ratio Abbreviation for *Price Earnings Ratio*.

Percentile   A statistical measure representing the ranking of a particular figure or outcome on a scale comprising 100 equal groups. (See also *Quartile*).

Performance Measurement   A form of analysis that attempts to compare investment manager performance. It can be critically affected by the time period selected and while some attempts have been made to look at risk adjusted returns, generally it is very difficult to assess the quality of those returns. Good performance measurement should include: a) analysis of performance over a *business cycle* (typically 3-5 years) and assessment of returns on a quarterly basis, ideally by sectors as well as total returns; b) ensuring that like is being compared with like – the best way to do this is to look at each manager's *benchmark*, or risk profile, and compare performance against the benchmark, preferably on a sector basis; and c) analysis of the reason for any extreme out-or-under performance in a given period (eg. whether a large *overweight* position exists in one or a few securities or a sector).

Personal Approved Deposit Fund (PADF)   An *Approved Deposit Fund (ADF)* with one individual as the investor. The portfolio is structured and managed to meet that individual's personal requirements and objectives.

Personal Superannuation Plan   An arrangement, often in the form of a policy from a life insurance company, under which individuals can make superannuation contributions without the need for employer contributions.

Physical Market a) The market in tangible assets such as plant and equipment, as distinct from markets in financial investments (ie. bonds, shares, etc); b) The term is also sometimes used to distinguish investments in *derivative* securities (futures or options) from the underlying ('physical') securities from which they were derived.

Physical Security See *Underlying Security*.

PI Cover See *Professional Indemnity*.

Pin Risk The risk to a trader who has sold an option that at expiration the price of the underlying security will be identical to the exercise price of the option. The trader, therefore, will not know whether the option is likely to be exercised.

Placement An issue of newly-created shares by a company which is already established, as a means of raising cash and/or diversifying its investments. (See also *Private Placement*).

Plc Abbreviation for public limited company, the term used in the United Kingdom to describe a company limited by shares (see *Company*). A company must be a Plc in order to be listed on the London Stock Exchange. (See also *Listed Company*).

Poison Pill An anti-takeover device used by a company to protect itself from hostile bidders. There are many varieties of poison pills, the most common being the 'flip-over', which guarantees the shareholders of a company targeted for take-over the right to purchase shares in the new, merged entity at below market cost, thereby reducing the raider's gain. (See also *Sugar-coated Pill*).

Policy The legal contract between an insurer and the insured individual/company/trustee, etc.

Policy Committee A committee, comprising equal representation from employers and members, which is established under provisions of the *SIS Legislation* to advise the trustees of a *Public Offer Fund*.

Political Risk The uncertainty in return on a foreign investment due to the possibility that the foreign government might take actions which are detrimental to the investor's interests.

Pooled Development Fund (PDF) A form of *pooled investment* which offers taxation concessions for investors to invest in development capital projects. To be eligible for PDF status, the trustees must submit a capital raising plan and investment plan for approval by the PDF Registration Board of the Commonwealth Department of Industry, Science and Technology. PDFs may only invest in Australian companies with less than $50 million in assets. As at April 1996, there were 36 PDFs registered in Australia.

Pooled Investment Any form of investment in which a number of individuals place their money with a professional manager to manage the total fund on their behalf and produce a return to them individually. Also known as **Collective Investment**.

Pooled Superannuation Trust (PST) A superannuation trust which complies with certain conditions set out in the *SIS Legislation* and Regulations, and into which *complying funds* may place their investments.

Portability In relation to superannuation, the ability to switch benefits from one fund to another, or from a superannuation fund into a *rollover* fund (eg. upon a change of employment).

Portfolio   The collection of investment holdings of a particular investor usually with reference to its composition – ie. the mix of different classes of securities, such as bonds, property, shares and cash, or if in a single *asset class,* the mix of different sectors and stocks.

Portfolio Construction   The process of identifying which asset classes to invest in, and in what proportions.

Portfolio Insurance   An investment strategy which aims to ensure a minimum rate of return while allowing the investor to benefit from the positive returns generated by investment in a risky portfolio. (See *Dynamic Hedging*).

Portfolio Manager   A person or organisation engaged to manage investment portfolios and make investment decisions on behalf of others.

Portfolio Optimisation   The process of selecting an investment portfolio that minimises risk for a given level of return, taking account of a) expected return; b) variances of expected return; and c) *covariance* of return with every other security under consideration.

Position   a) The total of an option trader's open contracts in a particular underlying security; b) A market commitment. For example, a purchaser of a futures contract has a *long position,* while a seller of a future contract has a *short position.*

Preference Shares   Shares which rank before ordinary shares in the event of liquidation of the issuing company and usually receiving a fixed rate of return on the unfranked investment. (See also *Ordinary Shares*).

Premium a) The opposite of *discount*; b) The amount paid at the time of purchase (eg. of an option); or c) a periodic payment made towards an insurance policy.

Prescribed Interest A statutory concept introduced in the *Corporations Law,* covering a wide range of collective investment activities administered by investment managers. Prescribed interests include: a) funds management activities, such as property trusts, cash management trusts and equity trusts; b) business investment projects, such as film investment schemes or certain agricultural schemes; and c) recreational investments, such as timeshare holiday apartments and horseracing syndicates. Prescribed interests are treated differently from other collective investments for certain regulatory requirements (eg. *prospectus* provisions).

Present Value The current value of an investment which matures in the future, after *discounting* the maturity at an assumed rate of interest and adjusting for the probability of its payment or receipt.

Preservation The maintenance of superannuation benefits and/or *eligible termination payments* in superannuation or *rollover* funds until retirement. Under current laws, some benefits are subject to compulsory preservation until retirement (ie. they must be preserved in a superannuation or rollover fund, and cannot be withdrawn beforehand). (See also *Vesting).*

Price-Earnings Ratio (PE Ratio) A stock's market price divided by its current or estimated future *earnings per share*; a fundamental measure of the attractiveness of a particular security versus all other securities as determined by the investing public. The lower the ratio relative to the average of the sharemarket, the lower the (market's) profit growth expectations. Also called **Earnings Multiple**.

Price Input The effect on the price of a security resulting from a trade in that security (eg. a major sale or purchase).

Price Range The range between the highest price and the lowest price reached by a certain security, or the general market, during any specific day, week or year.

Prices and Incomes Accord See *Accord*.

Prices Surveillance Authority (PSA) The former Commonwealth Government agency responsible for administering legislation concerning prices, and merged in 1995 with the *Trade Practices Commission* to form the *Australian Competition and Consumer Commission*.

Primary Market The market in which securities are sold at the time they are first issued. (Opposite of *Secondary Market*).

Prime Assets Ratio (PAR) A prudential requirement under which banks have to hold a prescribed percentage of the value of their total liabilities in specified highly secure assets. These currently consist of notes and coins on issue, balances with the Reserve Bank, Commonwealth government debt securities and loans to official dealers secured by Commonwealth securities.

Prime Rate The minimum rate on bank loans set by commercial banks. It is affected by overall business conditions, the availability of reserves and the general level of interest rates, and may vary geographically. Lending rates are also greatly influenced by the size of the loan; the largest loans naturally command the lowest rates. Also called **Base Rate**.

Private Equity An equity interest in an unlisted company or enterprise. (See also *Development Capital*).

Private Placement The *placement* of a security with an institutional investor or investors as opposed to a public offering.

Private Sector The part of the economy owned/operated by corporations and individuals outside the *public sector*. Split by economists into households and business.

Privatisation The alteration of the legal and management structure of a Government trading body (eg. a *statutory authority*) to permit private equity or ownership (as opposed to *corporatisation*, under which ownership and control remain with the Government).

Productivity The level of efficiency with which goods or services are produced given the inputs used to produce those goods and services.

Professional Indemnity A form of insurance against negligence or defalcation by a professional adviser (eg. a lawyer or an accountant). Also known as **PI Cover**. Investment managers and custodian companies generally take PI cover as well.

Profit and Loss Account A financial statement showing the earnings and expenses of a company over a given reporting period (as distinct from a *balance sheet*, which shows the company's assets and liabilities at a set point in time).

Profit Taking The act of selling securities which have appreciated in value to translate a *paper profit* into a realised gain. Often used to partly explain a market decline after a noticeable run-up in prices.

Program Trading a) A synonym for *index arbitrage*; or b) A synonym for *package trading*.

Promissory Note A *debt security* issued by a borrower, showing the amount which the borrower is prepared to pay the noteholder on its maturity. The note is issued at a discount to its face value, representing the *yield* on the funds for the noteholder (lender). Promissory Notes are similar to *Bills of Exchange* with the exception that only the name of the borrower and not the lender appears on the face of the note.

Proper Authority An instrument under the *Corporations Law* which signifies the responsibility of a securities dealer or investment adviser for acts of an employee or agent. Proper authorities are required to be provided to certain categories of employees of fund managers sharebrokers and investment advisers. (See also *Dealer's Licence*).

Property In the finance industry, the term refers to real estate including land and buildings that can be bought, sold or leased.

Property Trust A *collective investment* vehicle which owns a portfolio of real property, thus providing for a wider spread of ownership. **Listed property trusts** are quoted on the stock exchange, and their prices fluctuate with supply and demand, as with equity investments. Unlisted property trusts are transacted directly with the trust's manager, who fixes the prices in relation to the established asset backing of the trust, with adjustments for expenses.

Proprietary Limited Usually abbreviated to *Pty Ltd*. (See also *Company*).

Prospectus A legal document lodged and/or registered with the *Australian Securities Commission* setting forth the complete history and current status of a security issue or fund, and which must be made available to all interested investors in advance of their investment, when an offer is made to the public.

Protected Growth Fund An investment portfolio which aims to maximise growth to the greatest extent possible consistent with the objective of achieving a positive return for each financial year. (See also *Capital Protected* and *Growth Fund*).

Protection Overlay A portfolio management technique by which an investment manager aims to protect the capital value of a portfolio through risk management techniques, such as *dynamic hedging*.

Provisional Tax A form of income tax collection, normally levied on non-*PAYE* taxpayers such as self-employed professionals. Provisional tax is usually payable in April, prior to the end of the taxation year in question.

Proxy A written authorisation given by a shareholder to someone else to vote his or her shares at a shareholder's meeting. Fund management agreements often delegate the authority to the fund manager to exercise proxy votes on behalf of the client. (See also *Corporate Governance*).

Prudential Standard A regulatory control imposed on a financial institution to protect the interests of its depositors or other creditors (eg. a restriction on foreign currency transactions or on the maximum shareholding which can be held by a single individual or group). (See also *Capital Adequacy*).

Prudent Man Rule A common law standard applied by the Courts to the investment of trust funds. Briefly stated: 'All that can be required of a trustee in the investment of trust funds is that he conduct himself faithfully and exercise sound discretion. He is to observe how men of prudence, discretion and intelligence manage their own affairs, not in regard to speculation, but in regard to the permanent disposition of their funds, considering the probable income as well as the probable safety of the capital to be invested'. The Prudent Man Rule is tending to be replaced by the notion of the 'Prudent Expert'.

PSBR Abbreviation for *Public Sector Borrowing Requirement*.

PST Abbreviation for *Pooled Superannuation Trust*.

Pty Ltd A contraction of proprietary limited company, and a term unique to Australia, New Zealand and South Africa. See *Company*.

Public Offer Entities A legal term under the *SIS Legislation* for *Public Offer Funds*.

Public Offer Fund   A type of superannuation fund which, under the *SIS Legislation*, is required to comply with certain regulatory requirements, including the need to have a *corporate trustee*, to meet certain disclosure requirements and to establish a *policy committee* to advise the trustee directors. Public offer funds include superannuation products marketed directly to the public and master trusts, although other funds can obtain public offer fund status either by their own choice or by declaration by the *Insurance and Superannuation Commission.*

Public Sector   The part of the economy which is made up of Government (Commonwealth, State and Local) enterprises and activities. The public sector includes public service departments, essential services such as health, education, transport and defence and utilities, such as electricity and water authorities. (See also *Private Sector* and *Statutory Authority*).

Public Sector Borrowing Requirement (PSBR)   The amount of borrowing required (whether through issuance of bonds, increasing money supply or offshore borrowing) to supplement revenue so as to finance the activities of governments and semi-government authorities.

Purchase Price   See *Allocation Price.*

Purchasing Power   The extent to which a sum of money or benefit can retain its ability to purchase physical assets. Investors generally aim to improve or at least to preserve the purchasing power of their money or assets against increase in the inflation rate over time.

Put Option   An *option* giving its purchaser the right, without the obligation, to sell an asset at a specified price (the *exercise price*) at any time between the purchase of the option and its expiry date. (See also *Call Option*).

Quotation

Quant   Abbreviation for *Quantitative Analyst,* a specialist who engages in *quantitative management.*

Quantitative Management   An approach to investment management which seeks to use statistical or numerical methods to create efficient portfolios, with the optimum risk/return trade-off. Quantitative managers generally attempt to add value by exploiting pricing anomalies, or by providing particular levels of risk control, rather than by subjective forecasting of market behaviour.

Quartile   A statistical measure dividing a sample into four numerically equal groups. Thus, 'top quartile' means the top 25% of a given sample. (See also *Decile, Percentile*).

Quotation   Often shortened to 'quote'. See *Bid-Asked*.

Rally A brisk rise following a decline in the general price level of the market or an individual share.

Ramping The practice of transacting securities to generate a higher general level of market activity to drive prices upwards so securities can be sold at a higher price.

Range The difference between the highest and lowest prices recorded during a given trading session, week, month, year, etc.

Rate of Return The income yield earned in relation to a capital amount invested.

RBA Abbreviation for *Reserve Bank of Australia*.

RBL Abbreviation for *Reasonable Benefit Limit*.

Real Estate Property in land, building or housing, as distinct from personal property (eg. cars); also known as physical property to distinguish itself from *Property Trusts*.

Real Interest Rate The nominal interest rate less the prevailing rate of *inflation*.

Realise To sell an asset (usually when it appears to have appreciated to the maximum extent that can be reasonably expected).

Real Return An inflation-adjusted return. (See also *Nominal Return*).

Reasonable Benefit Limit (RBL)   The maximum benefit which members of superannuation funds are permitted by the Government to receive on a concessionally taxed basis either as on lump sum (**Lump Sum Reasonable Benefit Limit**) or a pension (**Pension Reasonable Benefit Limit**). From the commencement of the *SIS Legislation* on 1 July 1994, RBLs are set at a flat dollar amount for all retiring members (previously the limit was calculated by reference to the member's salary prior to retirement). More generous RBLs apply in respect of pension benefits than lump sum, reflecting the Government's policy of encouraging the provision of benefits as an income stream and reducing opportunities for double dipping.

Rebate   The return of a proportion of a payment which effectively reduces the total outlay or obligation.

Receiver   A person appointed, either by a creditor or by a court, to take charge of the affairs of a company until its debts are paid. The company is thus in *receivership*. (See also *Administrator, Liquidator*).

Receivership   The condition of a company that has had a *receiver* appointed to administer it. Unlike *liquidation*, receivership does not necessarily lead to cessation of the company's business.

Recession   A significant slowdown in the economy, but not of the same severity or duration as a *depression*. The term recession is sometimes used in a more technical sense to refer to a period in which a nation's *GDP* declines over two consecutive quarters.

Redeemable Preference Shares

Redeemable Preference Shares Shares which can be sold back to the issuing company on a specified maturity date for their face value plus dividend payments.

Redemption Fee A fee charged for the redemption (ie. withdrawal/cashing in) of units in a *unit trust*. Also known as **Back-end Load**.

Redemption Price The price at which an investor can withdraw his or her units in a *unit trust*. Opposite of *Allocation Price*.

Redemption Yield See *Yield*.

Rediscount Rate A repurchase or buy-back rate, set by the Reserve Bank (RBA) and changed from time to time in line with market rates. The RBA will rediscount or buy back *Treasury Notes* with a maturity date of less than 90 days; in times of tight liquidity authorised dealers and banks can generate cash by rediscounting notes.

Refinancing The practice by a company of retiring existing securities by the issue of new securities to save interest costs, consolidate debt or lengthen maturities, or some combination of these three goals.

Reflation Restoration of deflated prices to a desirable level. When Governments reflate, additional money is printed, adding to the supply of money in circulation.

Registered Traders Market makers in the *Exchange Traded Options* market.

Registry An accounting firm or other organisation engaged to issue shares authorised by a company.

Regression Analysis A statistical technique used to measure the impact (eg. on a share price) of a change in one or more variable factors.

Regulated Superannuation Fund A superannuation fund which falls under the regulatory ambit of the *SIS Legislation*. A fund becomes a regulated superannuation fund when it elects to adopt a *corporate trustee* structure, or when its principal activity is the provision of age pensions to its members. Although not compulsory, the transition to a regulated fund is necessary to achieve *complying fund* status and to be eligible for concessional taxation treatment.

Reinsurance The taking out of insurance to protect against risks to which the insurance company is not prepared to be exposed.

Relevant Interest A legal status applying to some share investors under the *Corporations Law*. A person has relevant interest in a share if he/she has the power to either exercise or control the voting right or power to dispose of or control the disposal of that share.

Repatriation of Surplus The payment of surplus from a *Defined Benefit* superannuation fund to the employer or sponsor of the fund. The circumstances in which repatriation of surplus may occur are usually set out in the Fund's *Trust Deed*, and are subject to certain provisions of the *SIS Legislation* (eg. a requirement that the Fund's members be given at least three months' notice of the return of surplus to the employer).

Replication See *Index Fund*.

Repurchase Agreement ('**Repo**') An agreement under which authorised dealers in the short-term money market transfer securities to the Reserve Bank in exchange for cash, on the basis that the transaction will be reversed at a later date on agreed terms. The transaction can also occur in the opposite fashion (**reverse repo**). The main purpose of these arrangements is to allow the Reserve Bank to manage *liquidity* in the money market.

Reserve Bank of Australia (RBA) Australia's central bank; came into being in 1959 when the central banking activities of the Commonwealth Bank of Australia were transferred to the new entity. The RBA's role combines that of guardian of the financial system and confidant to the Federal Government. It has responsibility for the banking system and *authorised dealers*, as well as overseeing the activities of Australia's financial markets.

Reserve Currency a) A country's foreign exchange account held by the Central Bank for the facilitation of the payments and receipts denominated in foreign currencies; b) A currency or commodity held as a safe haven, usually in US dollars and/or gold.

Reserves a) The proportion of a company's profit not distributed to shareholders as *dividends*; b) An account kept aside by the trustees of a superannuation fund to cover declines in asset values or investment returns.

Resource Shares Shares of companies engaged in mining, energy and commodity related activities, as opposed to *Industrial Shares*. These shares are classified as the Resource Sector in the *All Ordinaries Index*.

Retail Investment Products Investment funds that are structured to accept investments from individuals. These funds are pooled and invested by an investment manager. A number of different types of funds exist aimed at meeting the investment requirements of individuals. (Opposite of *Wholesale Investment Products*).

Retirement Savings Account (RSA) A proposed vehicle for *superannuation* savings, akin to a bank account, which could be selected by employees as an alternative to conventional superannuation funds. At the time of going to print (April 1996), the details of RSAs had not been finalised by the new Coalition Government. However, it is expected that they will be targeted particularly at part-time and casual workers who may be disadvantaged by the fee structure of conventional superannuation funds.

Return The amount of money received annually from an investment, usually expressed as a percentage.

Return if Exercised The estimated rate of return an *option* seller will gain as a percentage of the outlay in the event of it being exercised.

Rho The ratio of the change in an *option price* to a change in interest rates.

Rights Issue An offer made to a holder of an existing security to purchase new securities issued by the same company at a discount to the existing market, and able to be exercised within a relatively short (30-60 days) time span.

Risk In its simplest sense, risk is the variability of returns. Investments with greater inherent risk must promise higher expected yields if investors are to be attracted to them. Risk can take many forms, but a major one is *Valuation Risk* – paying too much for an asset. (See also *Currency Risk, Exchange Risk, Exposure Risk, Market Risk, Operations Risk, Political Risk, Volatility*).

Risk Aversion The tendency to require a relatively high return in order to compensate for risk, or uncertainty, in the result. Risk averse investors will tend to settle for a relatively low-risk portfolio, where the return is more predictable.

Risk Aversion Factor An expression of the degree of incremental return an investor requires to assume an additional unit of risk (or, conversely, the degree of additional risk the investor is prepared to assume to achieve a certain level of return). (See also *Capital Asset Pricing Model*).

Risk Capital Another term for *Venture Capital,* or, alternatively, capital which an investor is prepared to lose if an investment fails.

Risk-Free Asset An investment with no chance of default, and a known or certain rate of return. Typically in Australia the 90 day *Treasury Note* is used as a risk-free standard.

Risk-Free Rate of Return A theoretical return that is earned with perfect certainty; it is without risk. In Australia, the risk-free return is approximated by reference to 90 day *Treasury Note* yields.

Risk Management The monitoring and controlling of various risk factors in an investment portfolio with the aim of minimising volatility of investment returns.

Risk Premium The extra yield over the risk free rate demanded by investors to compensate them for holding a riskier asset. This is an extremely important concept in relation to setting a long-term asset mix. (See *Equity Risk Premium*).

Risk-Return Spectrum A concept used to illustrate that, in a rational marketplace, higher anticipated rewards are accompanied by incremental increases in risk (measured as the *standard deviation* of returns). The left end of the spectrum represents the lowest risk investments – typically short-term government securities. Moving to the right on the spectrum, each incremental increase in expected return is accompanied by an incremental increase in risk. (See *Efficient Frontier* and accompanying illustration).

Risk Weighting The assignment of percentage weightings to different forms of investments, reflecting their greater or lesser risks, for the purposes of calculating the *capital adequacy* standard to be observed by banks – eg. the risk weighting for residential lending is currently set at 50%, while for commercial lending it is 100%.

Rollover a) In relation to superannuation, the transfer of an *eligible termination payment* into an *approved deposit fund, deferred annuity* or superannuation fund prior to retirement in order to defer or (if the rollover remains in place until at least minimum retirement age) avoid the requirement to pay lump sum tax; b) In relation to banking, the renewal of a loan or extension of a deposit at defined intervals, normally including a revision of the interest rate charged or paid.

Rollover Payment Notification   A form which must be completed to notify the Tax Office and the former employer that an *eligible termination payment* is being rolled over.

Round Turn   A completed transaction in the *futures* market involving both a purchase and a subsequent sale or a sale followed by a liquidated purchase.

Royalty   Payment incorporated in the good or service's price which is paid to the owner of an asset (good or service) as compensation for its use.

RSA   Abbreviation for *Retirement Savings Account.*

R-Squared   The percentage of a portfolio's total return explained by market movements.

Rule of 72   A convenient technique for either mental or pencil-and-paper estimation of compound interest rates – derived from the fact that a 7.2% return per year is the interest rate that will double the value of an investment in ten years. Hence, 'years to double' an investment with a given annual rate of return can be estimated by dividing the rate of return into 72. For example, if an investment's annual return is six percent, its value will double in approximately 12 years (72 divided by six); if an investment's annual return is nine percent, its value will double in approximately eight years (72 divided by nine). Similarly, the rate of return that will double the value of an investment in a given number of years can be estimated by dividing the number of 'years to double' into 72. For example, the value of an investment will double in six years if the annual rate of return is approximately 12%.

Running Yield   See *Yield.*

Sale and Leaseback

Safe Keeping/Safe Custody   A service to customers rendered by trustee companies and specialist *custodians* for a fee, under which securities and other items of value are held for protection. Investment managers generally employ custodians to hold the assets of their managed portfolios.

Salary Sacrifice   The portion of pre-tax salary of an employee that is given up in exchange for additional contributions by the employer to the employee's superannuation.

Sale and Leaseback   A transaction in which the seller retains the use of the asset, such as occupancy of a building, by simultaneously signing a lease (usually of long duration) with the purchaser of the asset at the time of the sale. By so doing, the seller receives cash for the transaction, while the buyer is assured a lease, and thus a fixed return on his or her investment.

S&P 500 A United States stockmarket index, maintained by *Standard & Poors* (S&P), equivalent to the Australian *All Ordinaries Index*. (See also *Dow Jones Index*).

S&P 500 Index 1980-1995

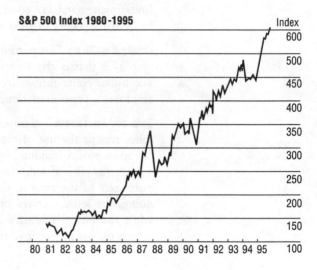

Scattergram   A graph illustrating the annualised risk and return performance of a fund or investment manager for a specific period (greater than one year). Risk is measured by *standard deviation* on the horizontal axis with return on the vertical axis. A point of risk and return for each fund or investment manager is plotted creating a number of scattered points.

Scattergram

	Return percent per annum
	Manager B 7
	6
• Manager D	
	• Manager A 5
Average Manager ⁄	4
	3
	• Manager C
	2
	1

Risk % per annum
2   3   4   5   6

In this hypothetical example of a scattergram the following observations can be made.

Each of Managers A, B and D have achieved returns above the All Manager Average; however Manager D has succeeded in achieving this at significantly below average risk levels. Manager B, whilst achieving the highest returns, has done so with the greatest risk of all funds measured. Manager C has achieved below average returns for above average risk indicating that it has performed poorly on both counts compared with the market.

Screening   Examination of various securities, usually through computer models, to identify certain predetermined factors such as valuations, earnings, liquidity, etc, with a view to the inclusion of those securities in an investment portfolio.

Scheme Operator   A responsible entity under the *Collective Investment Review* legislation.

Screen Trading   Trading of securities via a computer network rather than by open cry on the floor of the exchange. (See also *SEATS*).

Scrip   Abbreviation for subscription, or a certificate denoting entitlement to a parcel of shares. Synonymous with *Share Certificate*.

Seasonally Adjusted   Referring to figures or statistics which are modified to take account of seasonal factors. Employment statistics, for example, are seasonally adjusted in the first quarter of a calendar year to take account of the influx of school leavers into the workforce. The device is much loved in Canberra.

Seat   A traditional figure-of-speech for a membership of an exchange.

SEATS   Abbreviation for **Stock Exchange Automated Trading System**, the *screen-trading* system adopted by the Australian Stock Exchange.

SEC   Abbreviation for the (United States) *Securities and Exchange Commission.*

Secondary Market   Any market in which existing securities are traded (as distinct from the *primary market,* in which securities are first issued). The Stock Exchange is the secondary market for share trading.

Secret Commission   A profit or benefit received by an agent, from a third party, where the agent is dealing on behalf of a principal, without the knowledge or authorisation of the principal. The receipt of a secret commission is prohibited by law.

Sector   A group of securities that share common characteristics (eg. resources sector, textiles sector, etc).

Sector Range The maximum and minimum investment permitted in a particular sector in a *balanced* investment portfolio. An important aid for investors in ensuring diversification in managed funds.

Sector Trust A *trust fund* that only invests funds in a particular sector or segment of the Australian or international market. The investments of balanced portfolios operated by some fund managers are often held in the form of units in a range of different sector trusts.

Secular Trend A long-term trend either up or down in the price or level of a commodity, price structure, inflation rate, etc, which is not influenced by seasonal variations or distortions.

Secured Creditor A person or organisation which has lent funds on the security of specific assets of the debtor. In the event that the debtor defaults on its obligation the secured creditor may be entitled to have the assets in question sold to recover the debt. (Opposite of *Unsecured Creditor*).

Securities and Exchange Commission (SEC) The regulatory authority for the securities industry in the United States.

Securities Institute of Australia (SIA) The national professional body representing people engaged in and connected with Australia's investment and securities markets. Membership is drawn from a wide range of professionals including sharebrokers, merchant bankers, investment analysts, fund managers, bankers, investment advisers, securities dealers, lawyers and accountants. **Securities Institute Education** offers practical educational courses by lectures (in five Australian capital cities) or by distance education virtually anywhere in the world. Two courses are available: the Graduate Diploma in Applied Finance and Investment and the Certificate in Financial Markets.

The Institute also runs financial training workshop programs for people employed in the securities industry, including in-house training programs. The Institute's comprehensive Continuing Professional Development program includes seminars, luncheon speakers and corporate briefings.

SECURITIES INSTITUTE
OF AUSTRALIA

SECURITIES INSTITUTE
EDUCATION

Securitisation The 'packaging' of an income stream from selected assets and issuing of securities to investors backed by those assets. Securitisation enables relatively illiquid instruments (eg. mortgages) to be converted into marketable securities with active *secondary markets*. (See also *Mortgage-backed Certificates* and *National Mortgage Market Corporation*).

Security a) In relation to financial markets, the paper right to a (generally tradeable) asset. In this context the term includes *Bills of Exchange, bonds, share certificates* or any other interest-bearing paper traded on financial markets; b) An asset pledged to ensure the repayment of a financial obligation (eg. loan), and forfeited in the event of a default on that obligation.

Security Analysis a) The process of assessing the prospective future benefits of a security, the conditions under which those benefits will arise, and the likelihood of those conditions occurring or persisting; b) Examination of the value of assets put forward as security for a loan or other financial accommodation.

Security Valuation Model A model for calculating the price at which a security should sell. Typically based on the precept that the value of a security is the sum of the *present value* of the estimated future income stream.

Self-insured a) In relation to superannuation, referring to a fund which itself takes on responsibility for paying death or disablement benefits to its members rather than paying an external insurer to accept the risk; b) More generally, referring to companies who pay insurance premiums for their own business into a fund they directly control rather than using an insurance company to write a policy.

Seller's Market A condition of the market in which there is a scarcity of goods available, and hence, sellers can obtain better conditions for sale or higher prices. (Opposite of *Buyer's Market*).

Semi-Government Paper Fixed interest securities issued by a Semi-Government Authority, normally of greater than 6 months' duration, and often issued by a central issuing authority (eg. NSW Treasury Corporation). Of high credit standing, normally carrying a government guarantee. Often referred to as 'Semis'.

Sensitivity The amount of change in a variable produced by a given change in a factor input (eg. a change in *earnings per share* caused by a change in interest rates or A$).

Sensitivity Analysis A method of testing the responsiveness of an option price or indeed of any estimated outcome to changes in inputs.

Settlement In relation to share trading, an arrangement between brokerage houses for the payment or receipt of cash or securities. It represents the final consummation of a securities transaction and is handled through the stock clearing corporation.

Settlement Date The date on which the final consummation of a securities transaction takes place and payment is made.

Settlement Risk In relation to foreign exchange transactions, the exposure of one party to another on the value date of the contract. It is the risk that one party, having received settlement of one currency amount from the counterparty, is unable to effect settlement of the other currency amount.

SFE Abbreviation for *Sydney Futures Exchange*.

SGC Abbreviation for *Superannuation Guarantee Charge*.

Share The ownership of part of a company; a contract between the issuing company and the owner of the share which gives the latter an interest in the management of the corporation, the right to participate in profits and, if the company is dissolved, a claim upon assets remaining when all debts have been paid. (See also *Equity*).

Share Capital The capital of a company subscribed by its shareholders. (See also *Authorised Capital*).

Share Certificate A piece of paper representing legal evidence of ownership of a stipulated number of shares in a company. Also known as **Scrip**.

Shareholder The owner of one or more issued shares of a company who is normally entitled to: a) a proportionate share of the issuing company's undivided assets; b) dividends when declared by the directors; and c) the right of proportionate voting power.

Share Price Index An index measuring movements in the prices of shares, but not of their dividends (as opposed to an *Accumulation Index,* which measures movements in both price and dividend income).

Share Ratio A derivative contract developed by the Australian Stock Exchange in 1994 that allows investors to gain exposure to an equity, not on the basis of whether it goes up or down in price, but on the basis of its performance relative to *index*. Share ratios allow investors to hedge company *specific risk* during periods of potential volatility, because they do not pick the direction of the overall market, rather how a share will perform relative to it. At the time of going to print (April 1996), contracts were available for eight underlying shares.

Share Register   A register recording all of a company's shareholders and the number of shares they each hold.

Share Price Index Futures   See *SPI Futures*.

Sharpe Ratio   A statistical measure which attempts to show the performance of a portfolio's return in risk adjusted terms. It is calculated by dividing the portfolio's *excess return* over the *risk-free* rate by the risk (ie. *standard deviation*) of portfolio returns. The higher the Sharpe Ratio, the better the portfolio's return in risk adjusted terms. A Sharpe Ratio higher than one can be considered to be very good, while a ratio below 0.1 shows that the portfolio has been poorly rewarded for the risk undertaken.

Shelf Company   A company which has been incorporated, but has not traded.

Short Position   An excess of sales over purchases of a relevant commodity, currency or investment instrument. (Opposite of *Long Position*).

Short Selling   The sale of a security that is not yet owned, in the expectation that its price will fall so that it can be bought back later at a profit.

Shoulder   See *Head*.

SIA   Abbreviation for *Securities Institute of Australia*.

Simple Interest   The interest paid on the initial investment alone, as distinct from *compound interest*, which includes interest earned on previous interest payments as well as on the initial investment.

Sinking Fund   A fund into which a bond issuer makes periodic payments over the life of the bond in order to systematically reduce the amount of principal due on its expiry.

SIS Legislation   See *Superannuation Industry Supervision Legislation.*

Smaller Companies   Generally, companies listed outside the top 100 shares on the *stock exchange.*

Smoothing   The retention and application of *investment fluctuation reserves* to maintain a consistent crediting rate in a superannuation fund, notwithstanding volatility in the fund's actual earnings rate from year to year.

Snail Trail   A graphical depiction of a fund's risk and return performance over time, relative to industry averages. Risk (measured in terms of the *standard deviation* of returns) is measured on the horizontal axis, and returns on the vertical axis. The point where the two lines intersect in the middle of the graph represents the average risk and return of all funds surveyed within the sample. Against this matrix, the historical performance of a particular fund over consecutive time periods is plotted, and then joined by a line to create the 'snail trail' like plot. The preferable sector for a fund to be in is the top left-hand quadrant, which represents consistent above average returns and below average risk relative to the sample of managers or funds surveyed.

Snail Trail

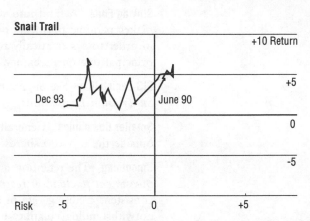

Snail Trail

+10 Return

+5

Dec 93   June 90

0

-5

Risk   -5   0   +5

In this hypothetical example of a snail trail, the fund depicted has moved, over time, from having above average returns with average risk followed by a period of increasing risk and return and, subsequently, a sustained reduction in its risk level with fluctuation (but always above average) returns. As can be seen, the fund has spent most of the period in the preferred quadrant of the graph, ie. top left hand quadrant, indicating above average returns with below average risk relative to the average manager.

Soft Dollars   Payment for research-related services by commissions generated from trading rather than fees.

Society for Worldwide Interbank Financial Telecommunication (SWIFT)   A non-profit *Electronic Trade Confirmation System* that provides secure messaging services and interface software to financial institutions globally.

Sole Purpose Test   The threshold test under *OSSA* and, subsequently *SIS Legislation,* with which a superannuation fund must comply in order to qualify as a *complying fund* and be eligible for concessional taxation status. The test requires that the fund be maintained for the sole purpose of providing its members with retirement benefits (or providing its members' beneficiaries or dependants with benefits in the event that the member dies before retirement). Certain other 'ancillary' purposes are permitted within the sole purpose test, including payment of disability benefits for a member's retirement due to ill-health or in other circumstances approved by the *Insurance and Superannuation Commission.*

Specialist Manager   An investment manager which confines its investment activity to specific asset classes (eg. equities, fixed interest, property, overseas shares, etc) instead of (or as well as) balanced funds. (See also *Balanced Manager*).

Specialist Sector Management   An approach to portfolio management involving the appointment of separate investment managers for individual asset classes, as opposed to the appointment of one or more *balanced managers* across all asset classes in which a fund is invested.

Special Situation   A term often used to describe an unusual investment opportunity due to either some special development or to perceived market mis-pricing.

Specific Risk Uncertainty in the return of a share arising from factors that are specific to the company concerned. It is unrelated, or, at most, distantly related, to events that impact on other comparable firms or the market as a whole. Unlike *market risk*, specific risk can be diversified away. (See also *Systematic Risk*).

Speculator One who is willing to assume a relatively large and generally undiversified risk in the hope of extraordinary gain. Speculators do, in fact, help give depth to securities markets. (See also *Investor*).

SPI Futures Abbreviation for *Share Price Index Futures*. One of the important futures contracts offered on the *Sydney Futures Exchange*. It trades around the underlying physical level of the *All Ordinaries Index*. The difference narrows the closer the contract gets to its expiry date at the close of each calendar quarter.

Split A division of a company's shares into a greater number of units by reducing the *par value* (where applicable) of each share. In the case of a $10 share, a four for one split would mean that four new shares would be issued for each old share at an 'after-split' price of $2.50.

Split Funding The use of more than one investment manager to provide diversification of management as well as diversification of styles and classes of investments. Superannuation funds often split their portfolios managers to improve their chances of meeting investment objectives and reduce risk.

Spot Commodity See *Cash Commodity*.

Spot Price The present *physical market* price of the relevant commodity, currency or investment instrument.

Spot Rate The present conversion price of one currency into another, being the exchange rate for immediate delivery (ie. within two business days) of currencies to be exchanged.

Spread a) In relation to share, bond and currency markets, the difference between the *bid price* and the *ask* (offering) *price*, incorporating both an estimate of demand and potential profit for the seller; b) In relation to *unit trusts*, the difference between the *allocation* and *redemption price* of units, as a result of transaction costs incurred in buying and selling the underlying securities which make up the value of the trust; c) In relation to *options* markets, the holding of a *long position* and an offsetting *short position*, usually in contracts with the same *underlying security* or asset.

Squeeze A situation in *futures* markets in which those who are in a *short position* cannot repurchase their contracts, except at a price substantially higher than the value of these contracts in relation to the rest of the market. A squeeze can usually be attributed to scarce supply of the underlying physical commodity.

SSN Abbreviation for *Substantial Shareholder Notice*.

Stag An investor in the share market who aims for quick gains by subscribing to new share issues and then selling once the shares commence trading on the exchange.

Stamp Duty A State Government charge levied on certain property and securities transactions.

Standard & Poors (S&P)   A United States credit rating agency. S&P also maintains a range of United States sharemarket indices; the most widely quoted is the *S&P 500*. (See also *Australian Ratings, Moody's*).

Standard Deviation   A statistical measure of the dispersion of a set of numbers around a central point. If the standard deviation is small, the frequency of distribution is concentrated within a narrow range of values. For a *normal distribution*, about two thirds of the observations will fall within one standard deviation of the *mean*. Standard deviation is a commonly used measure of risk because the higher the standard deviation the higher the uncertainty of the return. As standard deviation measures the *volatility* of investment returns, it is an important measure of risk. Also known as **Standard Error**.

Standard Error   Another term for *Standard Deviation*.

Statutory Authority   A public (or semi-government) authority established by legislation, and having the power to make legally enforceable decisions and regulations. Examples includes bodies responsible for electricity generation, gas, water supply, etc.

Statutory Fund   A fund established by Life Insurance Companies, consisting of life insurance policy holder funds. Two or more statutory funds often exist, with the **Number One Fund** being low risk and capital guaranteed, and the **Number Two Fund** and following funds being higher risk or equity linked.

Stock   A generic term for *equities* (shares) and, less frequently, *bonds*. (See also *Security*).

Stockbroker A professional person who buys and sells securities on behalf of others in return for a commission (or *brokerage*).

Stock Selection The selection of an individual security within an asset class. For example, stock selection in relation to equity investments is made after analysing the financial standing, future earnings prospects and valuation of the shares of the company concerned. Along with *asset allocation*, stock selection is a key way in which investment managers add value. (See also *Attribution Analysis*).

Stop A point in the market whereby a trade is automatically executed at that level. Usually relates to *futures* positions.

Stop Loss a) A client's instruction to a broker to sell in the event that a stock falls to a certain level; b) In relation to foreign exchange markets, **stop-loss trading** refers to a strategy under which foreign currency is sold when it falls below a certain level.

Straddle A combination of *put* and *call options* which provides a profit if there is a large fluctuation either way in the underlying asset.

Strangle A position in *option* markets consisting of a long (short) *call* and a long (short) *put*, where both options have the same expiration date, but different *exercise prices*.

Strategic Asset Allocation The composition of an asset mix within a portfolio, constructed with the objective of meeting the long-term liabilities of a fund, rather than being based on short-term views of relative performance of the various asset classes. Usually a *benchmark* is derived in this fashion. (See also *Asset Allocation, Tactical Asset Allocation*).

Stratified Sampling See *Index Fund*.

Strict Liability The legal liability that applies even where the act or omission in question is committed inadvertently and/or without the intent to fail to meet a duty or obligation.

Strike Price Another term for *Exercise Price*.

Strip Hedging Constructing a series of *hedges* to cover an extended period.

Subordinated Debt Unsecured bonds that rank behind other debt, but ahead of shareholders, in the event of liquidation. (See also *Mezzanine Finance*).

Subscription An agreement to purchase a certain offering, eg. a certain number of shares for a stipulated price. Such an offer is not binding unless accepted by the properly authorised representatives of the issuer.

Subsidiary A company which is wholly or partly owned by another company but which (unlike a branch office) is still a distinct legal entity responsible for its own tax, regulatory compliance, etc.

Substantial Sharehold Notice (SSN) A form of notification which must be completed by a shareholder once he or she exceeds a certain proportion of the shareholdings in a company.

Sugar-coated Pill A term that describes when a company persuades its shareholders to approve a contentious matter by combining it with an unrelated beneficial one (eg. combining a proposed dividend with a proposed alteration of shareholder rights). (See also *Poison Pill*).

Superannuation A means of setting aside funds during working life for use as retirement income, under a regulatory system which provides certain taxation incentives and prudential controls for the benefit of contributors.

Superannuation Complaints Tribunal A tribunal established under the *SIS Legislation* to conciliate and, if necessary, review complaints brought before it by individuals who are affected by decisions of trustees of superannuation or approved deposit funds.

Superannuation Guarantee Charge (SGC) A policy introduced in 1991/92 Federal Budget, providing that, as from 1 July 1992, all employers who fail to contribute a prescribed level and standard of contributions to complying superannuation funds on behalf of their employees are required to pay a charge to make up those contributions. The SGC is scheduled to increase to 9% by 1999, and to be complemented by a compulsory additional 3% employee contribution, to be phased in from the 1997/98 financial year. A further means-tested Government 'co-contribution' to match the employee contribution has also been foreshadowed to take effect from 1998/99 (although at the time of printing – April 1996 – it was unclear whether this co-contribution would be delivered as a cash contribution to fund members or in the form of a tax rebate). The combination of these measures will mean that, by the turn of the century, up to 15% of wages and salaries of Australian workers will be invested in compulsory superannuation.

Superannuation Industry Supervision (SIS) Act/Legislation
Legislation enacted by the Commonwealth
Government in 1993, and commencing on 1 July
1994 for the regulation, responsibilities and
activities of superannuation funds. The SIS
Legislation replaces the previous *Occupational
Superannuation Standards Act* and Regulations and
brings the industry under the sole supervisory
authority of the *Insurance and Superannuation
Commission*. (See also *Complying Fund, Public
Offer Fund, Regulated Superannuation Fund*).

Surplus An excess of revenue or income over
expenditure. (Opposite of *Deficit*).

Surrender Value The amount due to the policy
holder if a life insurance policy is cancelled and
cashed in, prior to the maturity date.

Swap An interest rate, currency or equity exchange transaction involving two parties. In the case of an **interest rate swap,** one party is obliged to pay a fixed interest rate to the other party in return for a floating interest rate. In the case of a **currency swap,** one party is obliged to make payments in another specified currency. In practice with an interest rate swap only the net flow resulting from the exchange takes place; that is, the net payment will flow one way or the other in a given interest period depending on the level of the floating rate. For a currency swap the net exchange is settled in one of the specified currencies. Where both floating rate and currency elements exist in combination, the transaction is generally described as a currency and interest rate swap. **Equity swaps** can involve a variety of different transactions (eg. swapping the return in one market for that of another).

A typical swap transaction

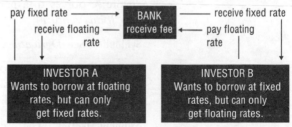

Swaption An *option* to enter into an interest rate *swap* transaction at a future date.

SWIFT Abbreviation for *Society for Worldwide Interbank Financial Telecommunication.*

Switching Facility The ability to transfer units between two funds or components of a unit trust – eg. between a *Growth Fund* and *Protected Growth Fund.*

Sycom   Abbreviation for *Sydney Overnight Computerised Market*, the after hours screen dealing system operated by the *Sydney Futures Exchange*.

Sydney Futures Exchange (SFE)   The main market in Australia for the exchange of financial and commodity futures. The Sydney Futures Exchange commenced operations in 1960 as the Sydney Greasy Wool Futures Exchange, and changed to its current name in 1972 to reflect its expanding role. (See also *Futures Contract, Financial Futures*).

Symmetric Hedge   A derivative position that protects the value of a specified percentage of a total exposure. The hedge is maintained at this level and only adjusted to the specified level for movements in the market value of the underlying assets.

Syndication   An arrangement between a number of different parties or financial institutions to jointly devote resources to a particular undertaking. (See also *Joint Venture*).

Synthetic   See *Derivative*.

Synthetic Option   An option position replicated by overlaying a varying position in the underlying asset with a partial holding of cash.

Synthetic Overlay   The use of *derivative securities* (particularly *futures*) by one manager (ie. the *overlay manager*) to reduce risk in another portfolio which may be managed by another fund manager. Equities and currency portfolios in particular lend themselves to overlay strategies. (See also *Currency Overlay, Protection Overlay, Tactical Asset Allocation Overlay*).

Systematic Risk   One of the components into which the risk of an asset, as defined by its price volatility, is usually divided – the other is *specific risk*. The systematic risk is the portion of the risk that relates to movements in the underlying market of which this asset forms part. Systematic risk is normally measured in terms of *beta*. It should not be confused with *systemic risk*.

Systemic Risk   Risk pertaining to the fundamentals of a system as a whole – eg. in the case of banking, the risk of failure of the Payments System or, in the case of property, a collapse of valuations owing to there being no buyers in the market. Systemic risk should not be confused with *systematic risk,* which relates to risks associated with individual securities rather than markets as a whole.

TAA Abbreviation for *Tactical Asset Allocation*.

Tactical Asset Allocation A process by which the *Asset Allocation* of a fund is changed on a short-term basis to take advantage of perceived differences in relative values of the various asset classes. A variation of asset allocation around a benchmark. (See also *Strategic Asset Allocation*).

Tactical Asset Allocation Overlay A portfolio management technique, managed on an *overlay* basis, which gains exposure to the same asset classes as the total fund, through *derivatives* rather than physical securities, with the aim of taking advantage of short-term movements and opportunities in the markets. Use of a tactical asset allocation overlay manager can allow for a fund to take advantage of that manager's asset allocation skills without them necessarily being responsible for ongoing management of the underlying assets. (See also *Overlay Manager, Synthetic Overlay*).

Takeover The acquisition of shares by one company in another so as to gain a controlling interest. Takeovers of Australian companies are regulated by the *Corporations Law*. (See also *Merger*).

Taker The purchaser of an option (in an opening transaction).

Target Company The company subject to a *takeover*.

Tariff A charge levied on imports with the aim of protecting local industries.

Tax Deductible Referring to an expense which can be offset against taxation liabilities.

Tax Exempt a) Referring to income which is not liable for tax in the hands of the recipient; b) Referring to a fund which does not incur tax on its income, by virtue of its beneficiaries being a specialised class of persons, eg. a superannuation *annuity* fund, or a charitable organisation.

Tax File Number (TFN) A number allocated to taxpayers by the *Australian Taxation Office*. The TFN is used by the Taxation Office to match income and taxation details.

Tax Loss A situation where total deductions exceed total income, based on the Taxation Office's definitions.

TCA Abbreviation for *Trustee Companies Association.*

Technical Analysis An approach to the analysis of stock and futures markets and their future trends which examines the technical factors of market activity, often represented by *charting* patterns, as contrasted with *fundamental analysis*. Technical analysts normally examine patterns of price change, rates of change, and changes in volume of trading and open interest, in the hope of being able to predict and profit from future trends. Some investment professionals are sceptical of the predictive ability of technical analysis, but most managers keep an eye on the charts anyway.

Technical Position A term used to describe the strengths and weaknesses of securities markets and individual securities as determined by specific criteria shown to have been reliable and useful in the past (eg. interest rates, money supply, inflation).

Technical Rally (or Decline)   Price variations, up (or down), arising from technical factors such as volume, open interest, delivery conditions or chart configurations, as opposed to movements resulting from supply and demand considerations.

Tender   a) The sale of a commodity or security through the seeking of written bids. (See also *Bond Tender*); b) A method used by governments to award contracts after publicly advertising their specifications.

Tender Notice   In futures markets, a notice announcing intention of tendering or delivering the actual commodity. A person with a bought futures position who receives a tender notice is usually required to take delivery.

Term Deposit   A deposit with a financial institution for a fixed period and a rate of interest which applies for the duration of the deposit.

Term to Maturity   The amount of time to elapse before the capital of a fixed interest security becomes due for repayment.

TFN   Abbreviation for *Tax File Number*.

Thematic Manager   An investment manager who utilises *macro economic* research and expertise to develop themes to influence its *asset allocation* decisions. The aim of thematic managers is to identify those factors in the market which will have strong influence on companies' profitability and on the market's perception of relative values.

Theoretical Value   An option value generated by a mathematical model given certain prior assumptions about the terms of the option, the characteristics of the underlying security, and prevailing interest rates.

Theta The ratio of a change in an *option* price to a small change in the option's *term to maturity*. In other words, the rate by which an option premium will decrease over time, all other things being equal. (See also *Vega*).

Thin Market A market in which there are comparatively few bids to buy, or offers to sell, or both. The phrase may apply to a single security or to the entire stock market. In a thin market, price fluctuations between transactions are usually larger than when the market is more active. A thin market in a particular share may reflect lack of interest in that issue or a limited supply of stock in the market.

Tick The smallest possible movement in the price of an asset. For example, the 'tick' size on a share in BHP is one cent.

Tick Value The dollar value effect of the smallest unit move in a *futures* or *option* contract price.

Tiger Economies A term for those Asian economies characterised by rapid growth and industrialisation since World War II. These countries include Taiwan, Singapore, South Korea and Hong Kong. (See also *Emerging Markets*).

Tight Money A condition existing when interest rates are high and credit is stringent, generally because of official control of interest rates and the money supply. (See also *Monetary Policy*).

Tilt The adoption of a particular view on a sector by *over-weighting* a portfolio in the direction of that sector, (eg. a portfolio with a high level of resource shares and low level of industrials would be described as having a resources tilt). Such a technique is commonly employed by *index fund* managers when clients indicate a desire for above-index returns.

Time Horizon The period of time over which an investment objective is to be realised. Time horizon is a critical factor for all investors in determining the types of investments they should make or, at least, the amount of risk they are prepared to carry. The investments made to provide for future retirement income, for instance, would almost always be different from those for short-term purposes.

Time Spread In options markets, a spread consisting of one long and one short option of the same type and with the same exercise price, but which expire in different months. All options must have the same underlying stock or commodity.

Time Value The balance of an *option premium* not represented by the option's *intrinsic value*.

Time Weighted Rate of Return A method of determining rates of return on the basis of measuring only the investment performance of assets held for the entire time period measured. This rate provides an effective standard for comparing the performance of different funds, in which cash flow could vary considerably. The investment manager usually cannot control the timing or the amount of contributions to the fund. Because the time weighted rate eliminates the impact of money flows into or out of the fund, it is a useful means of appraising the fund manager's ability to make the fund's assets perform. (See also *Money Weighted Rate of Return*).

Timing The art of deciding upon the exact moment to buy or to sell.

Title A document establishing ownership (eg. of real estate).

TN Abbreviation for *Treasury Note*.

Top See *Peak*.

Top-down Forecasting A form of security analysis which begins with forecasting broad *macro economic* trends then assessing the impact on industries and, finally, individual companies. (Opposite of *Bottom-up Forecasting*).

Topix Abbreviation for **Tokyo Price Index**. A Japanese share price index measuring share prices of selected large companies listed on the Tokyo Stock Exchange. Equivalent to the Australian *All Ordinaries Index*. Topix is a broader market index than the *Nikkei Dow Index*.

Total Return   The aggregate increase or decrease in the value of a portfolio resulting from the net appreciation (or depreciation) of the principal of the fund, plus or minus the net income (or loss) experienced by that fund during the period.

TPC   Abbreviation for *Trade Practices Commission*.

Tracking Error   The degree of proximity with which an actual portfolio follows a representative market index. Technically the tracking error is represented by the *standard deviation* of the differences in return between the portfolio and the index. Tracking error measures the likelihood (based on historical data) of actual returns differing from index returns.

Trade Practices Commission (TPC)   The former Commonwealth Government agency responsible for administering legislation concerning fair trade practices, and merged in 1995 with the Prices Surveillance Authority to form the *Australian Competition and Consumer Commission*.

Trader   A person who actively buys and sells securities for his or her own account, usually with relatively short time horizons.

Trade-Weighted Index (TWI) An index measuring the value of Australia's currency in relation to those of its major trading partners. The index is weighted to take account of the volume of trade conducted between Australia and the countries concerned.

Trade Weighted Index 1980-1995

Trading Advice A document that must be sent by a broker to a client immediately after each trade, confirming all details of that trade.

Transaction Costs Costs associated with managing a portfolio, notably brokerage costs and stamp duties.

Transnational Corporation Another term for a *multinational* corporation.

Treasury Note (TN)

Treasury Note (TN) A short-term debt instrument issued by the Commonwealth Government, issued on a *tende*r basis each week for terms of either 13 or 26 weeks. The Reserve Bank conducts the tenders, which are pitched in line with liquidity expectations over the period in which the notes have to be paid for, as well as providing liquidity for periods when it is most needed (eg. tax run-down periods).

Trend A persistent and pervasive direction, upwards or downwards, of commodities, prices, earnings, etc. over a period of time.

Trough A charting term, also known as a **bottom** (eg. in charting prices, a trough is the point where the price bottoms before the pressure to buy pushes it back up). (See also *Peak*).

Trust Deed An agreement spelling out the methods of receipt, investment and disbursement of funds under a superannuation plan, unit trust, charitable trust, etc. A superannuation trust deed will typically contain provisions for: investment powers of trustees, irrevocability and non-diversion of trust assets, payment of legal, trustee and other fees, liability of trustees, periodic reports by the trustees, records and accounts to be maintained, conditions for removal, resignation, or replacement of trustees, benefit payments under the plan, and the rights and duties of the trustees in case of amendment or termination of the plan.

Trustee a) A person or company that has legal responsibility for financial aspects (receipts, disbursements and investment) of funds; b) A trust company which acts in a capacity of trust as a *fiduciary* and to whom assets have been conveyed for the benefit of another party. The Trustee in this case oversees the behaviour of the manager in relation to the operation of a *unit trust.*

Trustee Companies Association of Australia (TCA) An industry association representing private state and public trustees since 1945. The main aim of the association is to represent the views of the industry to State and Federal government and regulators, mainly regarding legislation, and provide education to the industry and associated professions.

Trustee Director A director of a *corporate trustee.*

Trustee Investment Status A status conferred on selected investments by State Government Trustee legislation. Rules or trust deeds governing certain types of funds might require a portion of investments to be made in authorised trustee investments.

Trust Fund A fund whose assets are managed by a trustee or a board of trustees for the benefit of another party or parties. Restrictions as to the type of investments in which the trustee may invest the assets of the trust fund are usually found in the *trust deed* and in applicable legislation.

Turnover a) In relation to investment portfolios, the rate at which securities within a portfolio are exchanged for other securities of the same class; b) In relation to investment markets, the level of trading that occurs.

TWI Abbreviation for *Trade Weighted Index.*

U nbundled

Unbundled   Referring to the structuring of a product or service where the individual components involved in the management of that product are split out with separate fees usually applying. For example, an unbundled superannuation arrangement might involve separation of investment management, trusteeship and insurance arrangements among different parties. (Opposite of *Bundled*).

Uncalled Capital   That part of the company's issued capital which has not been paid for by the shareholders. (See also *Authorised Capital* and *Issued Capital*).

Undeducted Contribution   A component of an *eligible termination payment* comprising superannuation contributions (usually by employees) after 30 June 1983 for which no tax deduction was claimed.

Underlying   Referring to the stock, commodity futures contract, or cash index to be delivered in the event an *option* is exercised. The term underlying is often used as a noun in its own right, as well as an adjective.

Underlying Inflation   A calculated measure that takes the *headline inflation* rate and excludes certain volatile items or series that are affected by factors other than general economic conditions (eg. government taxes, or the effect of weather on fruit and vegetable prices). The resulting rate is based on only those items directly related to the economy.

Underlying Security   The shares, stock or commodity upon which a *synthetic* security is based. Also called **Physical Security**.

Underperformance Achievement of a lower investment return than a *benchmark* or other measure (eg. competitor portfolios) against which that return is being compared. (Opposite of *Outperformance*).

Undervalued Referring to a security or currency which trades below what is perceived to be its proper market value, taking account of statistical or fundamental research or other relevant information.

Underweight Having a lesser exposure to a particular sector in an investment portfolio, compared with a neutral or *benchmark* position. (Opposite of *Overweight*).

Underwriter A broker or bank which arranges the sale of an issue of securities on behalf of a client and, if it does not sell all stock to other institutions or investors, itself undertakes to purchase the unsold securities. By using an underwriter, the client is therefore assured of raising the full amount of money it is seeking.

Unfranked Dividends Share dividends paid by companies which are not subject to Australian tax (or paid by Australian companies, but before the introduction of *dividend imputation* in 1986). Recipients of unfranked dividends are subject to tax at their normal marginal rate.

Unfunded In relation to superannuation, describing a scheme in which the accrued benefits payable to members (ie. the liabilities of the fund) are not matched by the fund's current assets. Some Government superannuation funds have unfunded liabilities. (See also *Fully Funded*).

Unfunded Liabilities The actuarial calculation of the value of future benefits payable (eg. to members of a defined benefit superannuation fund) less the net assets of the fund at a given balance date.

Unit Trust A pooled investment fund or collective investment, established under a *trust deed*, that continually offers new units and stands ready to redeem existing ones from the owners.

Universe A term sometimes used to describe the total number of operators or competitors in a particular field, or the number of available stocks from which a portfolio is selected. Fund manager performance surveys are also referred to in this way.

Unlisted Referring to a company and/or shares that are not available for purchase or sale through the sharemarket.

Unlisted Securities Securities which are not listed on an organised stock exchange.

Unrealised Profits Profits which have not yet been received because, while the price of the asset has risen, the owner has not yet sold; ie. *paper profits*.

Unsecured Creditor A person or organisation who has lent money to another without taking *security* over specific assets of the borrower, so that repayment is dependent solely on the borrower's ability and willingness to repay. The lender is legally entitled to repayment but ranks after *secured creditors*, *debenture* holders, etc in the event that the borrower is wound up.

Upside Capture   A derivative structure in *capital protected* portfolios that minimises the potential for losses, whilst taking advantage of upward movements in a market or security price. The extent to which this structure benefits in overall returns when the market rises is called the upside capture. Usually the more robust the *floor return,* the lower the level of upside capture. (See also *Downside Protection*).

Up-tick   A small increase in the price of a security compared with the most recent transaction in the same security. (See also *Tick*).

Utility   A term used to describe the *statutory authorities* responsible for providing services to the community such as water, gas and electricity.

V alue Added Tax

Value Added Tax A term used in some countries for a *Goods and Services Tax*.

Value Date The trading date of the instrument being used to *hedge* an underlying exposure. This date is always before/the same as the underlying exposure's maturity.

Value Investor One who seeks to buy shares when they are underpriced and to take profits when they appear overvalued. The *Price/Earnings Ratio* is a key valuation measure.

Variance A measure of dispersion of returns on investments based on deviations from the average or *mean* value.

Vega The ratio of a change in the *option* price to a small change in the option *volatility*. (See also *Theta*).

Vendor A seller of an asset. In real estate transactions the vendor is the person disposing of the property.

Vendor Shares Shares that are issued in payment for assets sold to a company at the time of a float.

Venture Capital Capital which is subject to more than a normal degree of risk, usually associated with a new business or venture and particularly in relation to new technology projects. Also called **Risk Capital**. (See also *Development Capital*).

Vertical Integration The acquisition by a company operating in one market of another company which is complementary to its existing business (as a supplier or user of product) but which operates in another market eg. a newspaper publishing company acquiring a paper manufacturer. (See also *Horizontal Integration*).

Vertical Spread In *options* markets, a *spread* in which one option is bought and one option is sold, where both options are of the same type, have the same underlying security, and expire at the same time. The options differ only by their exercise prices.

Vesting In relation to superannuation, the inclusion of all or part of the employer contribution in the benefit payable to a member who leaves his or her employment (eg. resigns) before being eligible for retirement benefits. (See also *Full Vesting, Partial Vesting*).

Volatility The extent of fluctuation in share prices, exchange rates, interest rates, etc. The higher the volatility, the less certain an investor is of return, and hence volatility is one measure of risk.

Volume The aggregate number or value of securities traded during a given period.

Voting Right A right enjoyed by a shareholder to participate in the affairs of the company by voting at its annual meeting or other policy making forum. (See also *Corporate Governance, Proxy*).

W all Street

Wall Street The location of New York's financial district; most often used to refer to major participants in the United States sharemarket generally.

Warrant A certificate giving the holder the right to purchase shares of stock at a stipulated price within a specified time span, or in some cases, indefinitely. Warrants are sometimes attached to other securities as an added purchase inducement and may be traded separately after issue. They are similar to *call options*.

Wasting Asset An asset which declines in value over time. An *option* is a wasting asset because its time value will decay up until expiration day at which point the option value will be equal to only its intrinsic value.

Weighting The relative proportion of each of a group of securities or asset classes within a single investment portfolio. (See also *Overweight, Underweight*).

White Knight A friendly party in a takeover. The white knight 'saves' the target company from being controlled by an unfriendly aggressor by acquiring a block of shares in the company.

Wholesale Investment Products Investment funds that are structured and tailored for professional investors (including most superannuation funds, institutions and corporate investors) to invest in.

Withholding Tax The tax payable on payments such as dividends, interest and debt repayments, sent to foreign entities.

Write Down To reduce the recorded value of an asset in an account, eg. owing to depreciation.

Writer The creator, or seller, of an *option*.

Yield The return on an investment expressed as a percentage. Alternatively, the profit or income that an investment or property will return; the money derived from any given business venture, usually expressed as an annual percentage of the initial investment. Straight yield (or **running yield**) relates cash flow to price paid and does not take into account any gain or loss of principal. **Amortised yield** (or **redemption yield**) relates the sum of both cash flow (interest payments) over the life of the security and any gain or loss at maturity to the initial amount invested. (See also *Yield to Maturity*).

Yield Curve A visual representation of the term structure of interest rates. It shows the relationship between bond yields and maturity lengths. A normal or positive yield curve signifies higher interest rates for long-term investment, while a negative or downward curve indicates higher short-term rates.

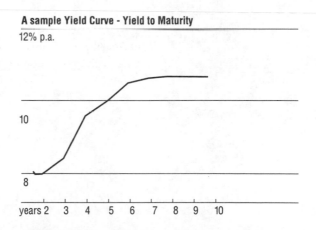

A sample Yield Curve - Yield to Maturity

12% p.a.

10

8

years 2 3 4 5 6 7 8 9 10

Yield to Maturity The *yield* provided by a bond which is held to its maturity date, taking account of both interest payments and capital gains or losses.

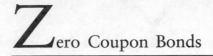

Zero Coupon Bonds

Zero Coupon Bonds Discounted bonds which are issued with no coupon, ie. there is no periodic income payment, and the yield to the bondholder is derived from the capital value of the bond at its maturity.